Globalization and Varieties of Capitalism

Also by Dan Coffey and Carole Thornley

INDUSTRIAL AND LABOUR MARKET POLICY AND PERFORMANCE: Issues and Perspectives

Also by Dan Coffey

CRISIS OR RECOVERY IN JAPAN: State and Industrial Economy (*co-edited with David Bailey and Phil Tomlinson*)

THE MYTH OF JAPANESE EFFICIENCY: The World Car Industry in a Globalizing Age

Globalization and Varieties of Capitalism

New Labour, Economic Policy and the Abject State

Dan Coffey
Senior Lecturer, Leeds University Business School, UK

Carole Thornley
Senior Lecturer, School of Economic and Management Studies,
and Director of Postgraduate Research, Institute for Public Policy
and Management, Keele University, UK

First published 2009 by
PALGRAVE MACMILLAN

Palgrave Macmillan in the UK is an imprint of Macmillan Publishers Limited, registered in England, company number 785998, of Houndmills, Basingstoke, Hampshire RG21 6XS.

Palgrave Macmillan in the US is a division of St Martin's Press LLC, 175 Fifth Avenue, New York, NY 10010.

Palgrave Macmillan is the global academic imprint of the above companies and has companies and representatives throughout the world.

Palgrave® and Macmillan® are registered trademarks in the United States, the United Kingdom, Europe and other countries

ISBN: 978–0–230–55309–5 hardback

This book is printed on paper suitable for recycling and made from fully managed and sustained forest sources. Logging, pulping and manufacturing processes are expected to conform to the environmental regulations of the country of origin.

A catalogue record for this book is available from the British Library.

A catalog record for this book is available from the Library of Congress.

10 9 8 7 6 5 4 3 2 1
18 17 16 15 14 13 12 11 10 09

Printed and bound in Great Britain by
CPI Antony Rowe, Chippenham and Eastbourne

*To the memory of Elfrieda Thornley
and Thomas Coffey*

Contents

Figures

Tables

Acknowledgements

This book is very much a joint effort. Dan Coffey is pleased to acknowledge the assistance of the Economics and Social Research Council, which funded some of the early research informing the latter part of Chapter 3 (via ESRC Award H5246006494), while Carole Thornley is pleased to acknowledge the assistance of the public-sector trade union UNISON for sponsoring and supporting much of the original empirical research on state employment which informs the analysis in Chapter 5. Other influences are acknowledged at appropriate junctures in the text, although we should perhaps follow the example of David Coates in his recent New Labour study (Coates 2005c: x) in acknowledging that general and major non-academic resource – the research journalism and commentary which informs this subject area. As per normal apologies to readers, the authors are pleased to accept as wholly their own all errors and omissions. Finally, our thanks go to our editors at Palgrave.

1
Introduction

There is a well known history textbook which commences its account of economic transformations in England with the anticlimactic observation that Britain is an island, a fact noted by its writer to be of contextual importance, even if 'not very original'.[1] It is no doubt just as uncontroversial to say that the advanced capitalist economies of today differ amongst themselves: Sweden is different from Canada, Germany from France, and the United States from Japan. Similarly, it would hardly excite controversy to say that the EU differs in its contested economic character from parts at least of what an able caricaturist would wish to highlight for North America, were regional rather than national state territories being compared. Debate over how best to describe and interpret such differences in economic organization within the world's advanced capitalisms as seem not only to coexist but also to persist over time is hardly new, however much the contexts within which the debate occurs changes; but the collapse of the Soviet Union with its satellite planned economies, and the clear emergence of aggressively state-backed capitalisms in the world's most populous nations, China and India, have given contemporary debates about differences in economic organization within mature capitalist economies a new kind of urgency and (for writers on the left) a particular kind of piquancy. The old speculations appear to have changed. The question, for example, as to whether European-style 'welfare state' models of capitalism would have evolved in the absence of an imminent threat to property from communism, has been replaced by the blunter issue of the future of welfare provision in an age when capitalism, to borrow from the title of the late Andrew Glyn's last work (Glyn 2006), is 'unleashed'.

1

This changed state of affairs provides context for the themes explored in this book, which seeks to contribute to the still-evolving debates over different models or varieties of capitalism by engaging with one advanced capitalism in particular. Our focal point in this connection will be on recent developments in Britain – or the United Kingdom – a selection which for a number of reasons is of comparative as well as of specific national interest.

Of immediate note is the fact that one common point of view, favoured by, but not exclusive to, writers on the political right, is that the United Kingdom is in microcosm emblematic, in its recent political and socioeconomic experiences, of a more general and decisive victory of liberal capitalism over socialism in the world at large. A typical reference point here – a conservative touchstone – are the Thatcher governments of 1980s Britain, which overlapped in time with Reaganism in the United States; this is a vantage point which takes us naturally to an 'Anglo-American' model of liberal capitalism. However, it is also true that in much of the literature concerning international economic positioning the United Kingdom is still treated as an entity balanced somewhere between America and Europe, reflecting both political orientations but also a still recognisably European welfare system. And combining elements of each of these anterior considerations, a range of policy commentators have now laid claim to the view that a new model of British capitalism began to emerge in the 1990s, evolving from, and with, the 1997 election of the first New Labour government (so-called) led by Tony Blair and his supporters.

One recurring theme here has been the invocation of a new type of balance, if not always consensus, within economy and society, combining a renewed commitment to a sustained and developing public services provision and a less neglectful social ethos than was evident under Thatcherism – supplemented by public-sector and welfare reform – combined with a pro-private business sector and market-led policy paradigm vis-à-vis questions of sustaining international economic competitiveness. On this last point, and resonating with contemporary concerns about globalization, the United Kingdom is by the standards of most international comparators an exceedingly 'open' economy – to trade, to short-term capital movements, to foreign direct investment, to foreign ownership; and much is made of the need to retain a hard-headed view of competitiveness in a global economy. The resignation of Tony Blair, ten years after his election, as prime minister, and the uncontested ascension to this position of his chancellor of the Exchequer, Gordon Brown, has done little to change – after an initial flurry of speculation – the main features of the attendant debate on the character of Britain's variety of capitalism; and the possibility that New Labour may soon give way to a resurgent Conservative party has added a further layer to this debate, but without transcending its basic terms.

In this book our general concern, and the question guiding the selection of materials assembled within, is to ask what *sort* of capitalism exists in Britain today. By so doing, we seek to contribute to two clearly related but somewhat separate debates: on the one hand, the debate over the character of New Labour Britain, and on the other, the international discussions making up the presently emerging 'models' or 'varieties' of capitalism literatures, which seek in diverse ways to compare different national economic trajectories and state economic responses for interpretative and policy reasons. It seems obvious enough that too sharp a distinction should not be drawn: writers like Anthony Giddens – who early on identified New Labour with a 'third way' in politics[2] – have always had an eye on a wider international audience, while some of the most acute of New Labour's critics – for example, David Coates or Colin Hay – have made substantial contributions in shaping the varieties of capitalism debate; and it is not hard to see in this regard a tacit dialogue between two levels of understanding and engagement, between the specifically national and the internationally comparative.

One immediate clarification is, however, necessary. As Hay (2005) observes, the particular word arrangement 'varieties of capitalism' is potentially confusing, since it is used both in a general and inclusive sense – to refer to the fact that differences in national and regional economies may persist over space and time notwithstanding that consensus broadly agrees the economic organization per se remains capitalist – but also to describe one particular contribution to the subject area as a whole; more specifically, to the framework of analysis suggested by Hall and Soskice (2001), which argues that there is a basic duality between types of capitalist economy (they are either of the type 'liberal market economy' or 'coordinated market economy') and that an appropriate conceptualization should look at the complementarities deemed to be essential to the forms of interaction between private firms and non-firm institutions. While we shall certainly touch on this specific contribution, and extant criticism of it, throughout this book we refer to 'varieties', or 'models', of capitalism in the first sense (employing for the specific Hall-Soskice framework the acronym 'VoC' (see Hay 2005: 106–7)). Our understanding of the varieties of capitalism literature and debate is wide-reaching with regards to contributions elicited and approaches taken – as per Coates (2005b), which surveys the emergence of a discernible movement across a range of academic fields toward a sustained investigation of the viability of different forms of capitalism.[3]

We now offer a few words about the themes to be pursued in the essays comprising the main body of the text of this book, and our orientation to its subject matter.

Our starting point is with a shared premise in several recent major contributions to the worldwide debate over global capitalist trajectories. We have already referenced Glyn's (2006) *Capitalism Unleashed*, a study of the collective experiences of the advanced capitalisms of the Western and Asia-Pacific economies, focusing on developments since the ending of the long boom following the Second World War. Glyn's point of departure in this regard is to draw a contrast between the rising inflation, falling business profitability, comparative trade union strength, and confident left-wing movements of forty years ago, and the situation as it seemed to exist in the new century – 'low inflation, quiescent industrial relations, freedom for capital to chase profitable opportunities without restraint and the domination of market based solutions' (Glyn 2006: vii). Our second major reference in this connection is Naomi Klein's (2007) *The Shock Doctrine*, an almost spectacularly bold thesis about the exploitation of economic and social crisis – real or manufactured – as the basis for the pushing through of radical right-wing agendas across the world, of a 'neo-liberal' complexion. In each there is a common premise that the 1980s saw a sharp movement within Anglo-American capitalism in particular against the grain of post-war social and economic development. And although both writers draw on a broad canvas, in each the experience of Britain also looms large: Glyn's reflections on the augers of a new age in the 1980s – of monetarism, de-regulation, and privatization – are written with the British case very much in mind; and while some controversy has attended Naomi Klein's thesis that Mrs Thatcher's great achievement was to parlay victories over enemies 'without' and 'within' into a 'major leap forward' for a 'radical economic agenda' (Klein 2007: 138–9), even inimically minded readers may agree with her prognosis that this agenda proved to be a very substantial one. We explore the shared premises in each of these contributions, while sketching a basis for an interpretation of the emergence of Thatcherism which teases out an important distinction.

Against this backdrop, we consider how state policy in Britain today displays itself in various guises: in its response to powerful and mobile transnational corporations; in its dealings with profit-seeking businesses in the provision of public-sector services; and in its own role as an employer – by far the largest single employer in the country. We do so via a set of studies, dealing with topics that would in any case be of substantial independent interest from the viewpoint of economic policy, but which also serve another purpose given the overarching themes and concerns of this book. In each case the subject matter is chosen because of its potential to serve as a vehicle by which to understand what manner of state we are dealing with in Britain today. Economic policy – like social policy – is a multifaceted thing; rather than 'model-build', we further our inquiry into the character of the state by considering how it presents itself on key issues – mindful of the difference between what the state claims and what it actually does. This gap, between claim and evidence, rhetoric and reality, is a running theme in our book.

A further word is perhaps needed on our selections, in this regard. It might seem obvious enough, given the amount of ink already expended on these subjects, why we should elect to make studies of the state vis-à-vis its dealings with transnationally mobile corporations on the one hand, and its interface with the private sector on the other. But why include a study of the state in its particular role as an employer? One good reason, easily overlooked if one has never thought about it before, is that state sectors the world over are typically very large employers, much larger (say) than individual firms. Thus, and notwithstanding the 'shrinkage' of the state through privatizations, it remains the case that two of the largest individual employers in Western Europe today are each parts of the British state sector – in health (the NHS) and in local government. But there is another reason too, and one which is both fundamental and profound: in the United Kingdom, and again as with state sectors around the world, the public sector is characterized in its employment features by a highly feminized and extremely gender-segregated workforce. The state's cost imperatives vis-à-vis its own employees acts as a constraint on its policies on the regulation of employment more generally; and internally, the British state – as with state sectors elsewhere – is a major source both of low pay, and of unequal pay.

But if one looks, for example, at the 'concepts of explanation' characterizing main contributory traditions to the varieties of capitalism literature – as recently and valuably surveyed by David Coates: markets, production functions, patterns of cumulative causation, technology capabilities, social compatibilities, social embeddedness, class, modes of production, and so forth (see Coates 2005b) – it is hard not to be aware that these are traditionally employed in ways which either exclude gender as a relevant issue at the point of construction, or at best incorporate gender roles as an added point of note; as a complication, or as a footnote perhaps, but not as a principal issue. In this respect, it is not unfair to say that there is no systematic attempt to consider the differential experiences of women as a point requiring substantive explanation in the emerging varieties of capitalism literature; while one could hardly expect every contribution to deal with this issue, it should certainly be in there as a principal theme. The risk otherwise is of an oddly de-gendered worldwide debate: with women featuring, if at all, as the modern equivalent of the rustic props carefully included in those eighteenth century landscape paintings which took great care otherwise to keep the massed armies of field labourers out of the picture – inclusion might signal the social sensitivities of the artist, a box to be ticked 'done', but hardly amounting to a substantive study.[4] The particular selection made with regard to the state in its own role as an employer – massively important, if often overlooked – pushes comparative gender issues centre-stage.

And the inclusion of 'comparative' in this last coupling is real: in each of the studies comprising the text of this book, the 'global' emerges in definite if sometimes surprising ways – and not least in connection with the capitalist state as a 'model employer'.

From here we then consider the New Labour project – as it presents itself, on its own merits, and vis-à-vis the varieties of capitalism debate – in light both of our own studies and those of leading contributors to this rapidly growing subject; and then we consider the fact, intruding, unwelcome, but ineluctable, of the great economic crisis which has prompted outgoing President George W. Bush to nationalize sections of the US financial system in order to save it from disappearing altogether, and caused even the most Blairite of New Labour ministers in Britain to discover an activist role for the state. Again, we focus on precepts and actions, on what is said and what is done. And our aim throughout is to learn about the character of the British state in its guise as an economic actor, historically rooted, subject to pressure, but capable of independent action.

While to go further at this point risks crossing the line separating an introduction from a conclusion – individual chapter themes are set out below – we should perhaps be clear from the outset what this book is not about: it is not about Labour party organization, or the peculiarities of Britain's parliamentary constitution; nor does it contribute to the study of political demographics and psephology. An ample literature on these themes, even if narrowly restrained to aspects of the New Labour debate, exists; but it is not a goal of this book to contribute here – even were we qualified to do so. Nor is it about providing 'knocking copy', either of the New Labour project or of Mrs Thatcher, or for that matter of Old Labour or David Cameron. Lively critiques of New Labour as the big business party – David Osler's (2002) *Labour Party PLC: Party of Business* – exist, but again the form of our book, the purview of the materials within, have a different intent.

One last comment is called for: any work cited in the book which follows, even where we are in disagreement with the views presented within, is selected either for its representative quality, or its elegance or pertinence as a contribution. This is no less true for those contributions which differ from ours in their take on the issues.

An overview of chapters

We now follow convention by giving the reader an overview of chapter themes, with some brief accompanying comments on overall progression.

In Chapter 2 ('Globalization and Capitalism Unleashed') we develop several themes, each important from the viewpoint of setting the stage for subsequent chapters. First we provide a précis of the argument that both the New Labour project and Britain as a variety of capitalism can only be understood in the context of the traumas to which the economy was subjected in the 1980s, when alternatives to 'free' market imperatives across swathes of the economy seemed utterly crushed by the aggressive state policy platforms of the Thatcher governments; we focus, in particular, on the impact on organized labour and the vicissitudes of the trade union movement in this period. Noting the increasing reliance during this period of government on making the United Kingdom an attractive venue for transnational firms capable of investing elsewhere, we next step back and consider the implications – both for Thatcherism and the subsequent trajectories of British economic policy debates and practices – of the earlier destabilizing effects of transnational production activity in the 1970s, as a series of large companies operating in the United Kingdom extended and developed their European theatre of operations. By this means we establish the value of maintaining an awareness of international positioning when looking to understand developments impacting within the borders of national economies, while deepening and extending current debate on the 'shock' effect of Thatcherism. Finally, we close with some remarks on the claim that the recent evolution of capitalism betrays a transitionary process, from a Fordist state to a post-Fordist one.

In Chapter 3 ('The Commanding State') we consider the complex production politics of competitiveness when government makes support for capital mobility an express part of a strategy for attracting investment from large transnational corporations, and where workers' representative organizations then have to live with the consequences. This theme is pursued via a forensic reassessment of the circumstances that led Ford Motor Company to withdraw all Ford-badge car assembly operations from Britain, some decades after it moved to fully develop an integrated theatre of European operation. In the course of stripping back the multiple layers of this complex case we are quickly drawn into a world in which corporate decisions impacting on national economies cannot be understood except in the context of the wider strategic positioning of these firms. Our point of entry is the evidence taken and findings of a parliamentary investigation, an appraisal of which sheds new light on how a transnational firm exploits its 'reach'; and as we probe deeper into the Ford controversy, issues of race as well as class are encountered. But our principal concern is to ask whether Parliament or the state apparatus in Britain is willing to engage critically with the negative consequences of government policy positions that rely heavily on the respect the United Kingdom commands as a 'porous' economy.

The subject matter of Chapter 4 ('The Self-Effacing State') is contextualized by the pronounced policy shift favouring privatization in Britain, in which regard the United Kingdom has stood now for several decades as a world policy leader and fashion-setter. We focus on the latest wave of controversy on the steady movement to the private sector of functions previously organized by the state, via the so-called Private Finance Initiative (PFI), wherein private firms organize not only parts of the management activities of major public-sector projects but also initial investment funding through private finance. In the context of a wave of voluble and critical commentary, and in light of the underwhelming evidence vis-à-vis the benefits to the UK public of earlier privatizations, we look at the private finance debate from another perspective: we propose that this kind of financing initiative offers a unique opportunity – akin to a laboratory experiment – to gauge just how far the British state is willing to go in claiming its own incompetence. We ask if such a self-effacing state is rational; and if rational, what sort of rationality it is.

In Chapter 5 ('The Self-Deceiving State') we turn to the state in a third guise, this time as seen in the perspective of its attributes as a 'model' or 'good' employer when it comes to its own workers, and compared to employers in the private sector. But as we show, an assessment of this claim quickly carries us into deep and murky waters. We begin by exploring its roots in the cooperative and private sectors, before highlighting its worldwide prevalence and use by state sectors across the globe; we parse the developing terms of this concept in the specific but illuminating case of the United Kingdom, in both its historic and current contexts; and we consider the realities as to how the state actually discharges its obligations as an employer, a major if badly neglected issue for critical public policy research. We see too how the imperative of restraining wage costs in a relatively well-unionized and labour-intensive public sector segues into policy thinking on the regulation of terms and conditions of employment more generally; and we ask how the public advocacy by successive British governments – not least New Labour – of policy measures to advance equalities at work square with the realities of state employment distinguished, not only by its relative size, but also by the extent of its gender segregation and its low and unequal pay, and with internal and international pressures to liberalize public services. In these and other connections we consider the roles played in state policy thinking by self-legitimation and self-deception.

We have already intimated something about the light shed by each of these studies on a major facet of the British state in its contemporary guises as a policy maker, and about how more global considerations – again, in different guises – will appear at each turn. The remaining chapters explore themes of interpretation, and of pressures for continuity and change, with the current global and financial crisis imposing itself sharply.

Chapter 6 ('New Ways or the Abject State') considers Britain more broadly as a variety of capitalism, and explores two parallel debates: one UK-centred and focusing in upon the premises and consequences of the New Labour project, the other dealing with the complex question of how best to understand differences in space as well as time in the forms of economic organization displayed by recognisably capitalist economies. Taking New Labour on its own terms, as a commanding state, committed to capital mobility and labour market flexibility as necessary conditions to be fulfilled if competitiveness in world markets is to be maintained and growth potentials realized, yet leavened by a concern to sustain a modern public sector with a sizeable welfare provision, we consider 'third-way thinking' – both as a particular kind of ideological reflex and on its merits. At every stage in the controversy over how best to interpret New Labour's claims to distinction appeals have been made to comparisons with institutions and policy predilections in capitalist economies around the world; and it is clear, moreover, at least if we consider the period prior to the economic and financial crisis now enveloping Britain as elsewhere, that the policy precepts of New Labour – at least as theorized by admirers – have not infrequently been couched in terms implying the discovery of a superior good, for export. We explore the fact of New Labour from the point of view of what an assessment of this 'fact' brings to our understanding of the character of British capitalism, and what in turn this understanding can contribute to the form as well as content of the varieties of capitalism, and also 'employment regimes', debate.

Chapter 7 ('The End of Things') broaches a topic sprung by recent developments. The financial crisis rudely interrupted speculation, of the type that defies experience, that liberalized market economies are dynamic in consistently positive rather than complex ways. Of considerable embarrassment to the New Labour government – 'no more boom and bust' – we note the tendency to reference this as a 'global' phenomenon; and we consider the extent to which the crisis was internally generated because of particular economic policies pursued, with other policies neglected owing to particular mindsets prevailing. In each respect, we develop themes laid down in the preceding chapter. While events are still unfolding, we consider the end of things: the emerged responses, the questions posed for New Labour, and for wider global analyses of capitalism.

Chapter 8 ('Strange Days') concludes with some remarks on the book as a whole, why it is constructed as it is, and what insights it brings to critical assessment of the United Kingdom as an international role model, as a variety of capitalism, and as a putative third way.

2
Globalization and Capitalism Unleashed: The Travails of Labour

We must naturally be concerned with major changes to the UK economy in the years prior to the election of the first Blair government, and with how these impacted on the British labour movement, if we are to understand New Labour as a political project or developments in economic policy thinking more generally. This also becomes essential if we are to seriously consider likely future trajectories in the United Kingdom, or to appreciate some of the dramatic turns in policy now being undertaken in response to the collapse of the housing market bubble and the global financial crisis. Several notable works appearing in the past few years have emphasized not only the radical changes undergone prior to the first Blair government, but also have treated these as reflecting in a particularly aggressive form transformations evident in policy perspectives and contexts across many of the of the world's advanced capitalisms. Moreover, it is natural to commence with the dislocations conjured by the word 'Thatcherism' – some of the consequences of which are today explicitly accepted and at times seemingly endorsed by the parliamentary leadership of the Labour party as much as the Conservatives. For example, the decline of trade union membership and strength and loss of morale in these years, of profound significance to the subsequent course of British politics, often appears to be regarded retrospectively as both welcome and necessary.

In this chapter, our principal aims are several. We provide a précis of the 'shocks' to which organized labour was subjected in the decade now indelibly associated with Mrs Thatcher – the *Sturm und Drang* years of the 1980s – including in this connection the extent of the changes to employment legislation, the impact of mass unemployment and the increased tempo of de-industrialization, as well as privatization of public enterprises and outsourcing of provisions for public sector services. Thatcherism, and by implication some features of the New Labour project, in its determined assault on the position of trade unions in Britain, is often rationalized by an appeal to the industrial disease said to have afflicted the UK economy in the 1970s, frequently illustrated by means of casual asides on inefficient working practices and struggling firms. We deepen the terms of reference brought to bear on the traumas of these years by noting a contrary view scarcely admitted to in today's conventional wisdom, which is that large profit-seeking corporations – in the 1970s – destabilized key parts of the UK economy in the course of efforts to develop a regional (European) theatre of operations. We ask if this fostered an invidious perception of trade unions in Britain, and an exaggerated sense of the comparative inefficiencies of some of the key corporate players of the day. This provides a context in which to better locate the later shocks of the Thatcher period. It also allows us to better understand the evolved terms of one of the major policy debates of today informed by concerns over the global positioning of Britain's economy, namely whether labour market deregulation and other market-friendly reforms have enabled it to better measure up to the exacting standards of international competition.

While these are the main issues with which this chapter is concerned, we close with a brief address of one final theme. It became popular, from the mid-1980s, to argue that the dislocations evident in Britain's economy and society reflected an important change in the economic and cultural basis of mature capitalism more generally, and with specific regard to fundamental constitutive relations of production and consumption. Influenced by strands of literature appearing (initially and principally) in the United States and France, it was proposed – and still is – that a 'Fordist' form of mass production, imposing to varying degrees upon the economies of North America and Western Europe, was giving way to a post-Fordist sequel, reflecting and promoting wider societal transformations. We pause to consider this theme, less as a substantively convincing explanation of shocks to the system, but rather as a peculiar kind of intellectual response. However, we arrive at this point at the end; we begin by first considering some of the shocks in question.

Shocks to the system: the travails of organized labour

As observed in the introduction to this book, some notable works have appeared in the course of the past few years that emphasize the radicalism of transformations in the context and practice of economic policy in the world's advanced capitalisms. These compare the 'golden age' of the 1950s and 1960s growth boom with the policy prescriptions that began to emerge in the 1970s as growth stuttered and social stresses in America and Western Europe vis-à-vis the economy became apparent, and they also employ policy trajectories in Britain as a prime case in point.[1] The 'huge shift in economic policies and behaviour' observed by Glyn (2006: vii), is heavily weighted by UK examples; and Britain, under Mrs Thatcher, looms large for Naomi Klein, for whom was enacted, under conditions and by means which further destabilized the British economy and institutions, a 'radical capitalist transformation' (Klein 2007: 137). The British labour movement, most particularly its trade union wing, experienced the measures now forever associated with Thatcherism as something new and ferocious; a sense of the dislocation – Klein's 'shock' – is important.

There is wide consensus that the Conservative governments holding office prior to the election of the first Blair-led government in 1997 enacted policies reflecting a profound shift in labour market ideology and employment practice. As is well known, these years, first under Mrs Thatcher (from 1979), and then John Major (from 1990), saw substantial developments in employment legislation, in the composition and disposition of the national workforce, and in industrial relations. The cumulative impact in many areas proved very significant, and insofar as the position of organized labour and the trade union movement was concerned, the changes were negatively reinforcing.

If we consider employment legislation, a series of Employment and other Acts, backed by numerous statutory Codes of Practice, combined to legally restrict industrial action, eradicate the closed shop, regulate internal union government, dismantle statutory support for collective bargaining, and curtail individual employment rights. No less than five separate Employment Acts were enacted over the period 1979–1990, covering more or less the span in office of the governments led by Mrs Thatcher; along with the Trade Union Act of 1984, the Wages Act of 1986, and then (under John Major) the Trade Union Reform and Employment Rights Act of 1993. The extent and scope of this legislation, the persistence with which successive waves of it passed rapidly through a parliament dominated by large Conservative majorities, as well as its general tenor, is remarkable when viewed in its twentieth-century context. The cumulative and combined effect was to reduce the power of organized labour and to overturn previous 'welfarist' measures. With respect to direct wages legislation, for instance, the effect was to cumulatively repeal or rescind extant provisions for the protection of workers whose bargaining position with employers was known to be weak (see Thornley 2003: 84–6). Despite some countervailing pressures from European legislation, and occasionally misfiring efforts, as with requiring unions to ballot on political funds, the direction was clear: 'the law helped to change the conduct of industrial relations, and the reduction in employment protection…plainly gave employers more power' (Edwards et al. 1998: 18; also ibid.: 13).

This legislation was introduced in a decade of high unemployment, which pressed heavily not only on the bargaining power of labour but also the ability of unions to resist the onslaught. Unemployment complemented the anti-union laws. In the 1980s the trade union redoubts of manufacturing and mining and heavy industry more generally – steel, shipbuilding, the car industry, coal – suffered massive job losses, with badly decreased chances for newly unemployed workers of finding work without, and loss of union membership, job security, and labour market standing within. Unions achieved early partial successes in some of the more large-scale industrial actions of the period. For example the nurses pay dispute which erupted in 1981: the ensuing industrial unrest lasted through most of 1982 (see Thornley 1996: 166–8) – but major confrontations like the great miners' strike of 1984–1985, and the later printers' dispute at Rupert Murdoch's Wapping plant, ended with crushing defeats for the strikers.

An exacerbating factor not only insofar as rising unemployment was concerned, but also from the viewpoint of labour movement perceptions of the agendas now being pursued by a very right-wing government, was official policy adherence by the Thatcher government in the first half of the 1980s to the macroeconomic tenets of monetarism. A previous reliance by the Labour governments of Wilson and Callaghan on incomes policy as a means of bringing price inflation under control following earlier rises was abandoned; the new policy stance claimed that the key to inflation lay with the money supply.

To this end the real costs of borrowing were pushed up sharply between 1979 and 1982, leading to a sharp appreciation of sterling against other currencies and badly undermining the ability of British-based businesses to export profitably – causing a 'ferocious squeeze on manufacturing' industry (Glyn 2006: 27; also 25–9). At the same time, Geoffrey Howe, then Mrs Thatcher's Chancellor of the Exchequer, and in the midst of an economic downturn, reduced government spending – 1981 saw the budget deficit decline, despite falling tax receipts, as a result of cut-backs (see ibid.). The result of these measures was a very severe recession. The accompanying rise in unemployment generated a running controversy as to whether monetarism, which proved to be a relatively short-lived experiment as money supply targets proved impossible to hit, was simply an excuse for mass unemployment.[2] While unemployment had risen in the 1970s as compared with the previous several decades, the sharp increase now – unevenly distributed by regions of the country as well as sectors of the economy, and afflicting in particular male manual workers – was of an entirely different order.[3] It remained at very high levels, standing at rates of over 10 per cent for the larger part of the 1980s, and rising again, after a brief fall, in the first half of the 1990s.

Viewed in the round, 'shock' seems an appropriate enough metaphor, the more so when considered in connection with the rolling programmes of privatization, liberalization, and public-sector outsourcing that developed in expanse and scope over the course of the 1980s and into the 1990s. Privatization tended to replace national bargaining with company-level arrangements. Compulsory competitive tendering – a public sector outsourcing initiative – took workers outside of existing collective agreements and weakened the bargaining position for those that continued to be employed 'in-house'. These years were also years in which the decentralization of public sector pay became a major theme (albeit fiercely resisted) (see Thornley 2003: 85). Glyn's summary judgement upon privatization experiments worldwide, that the 'main losers' are typically 'workers who [lose] relatively well-paid unionized jobs', can be noted (Glyn 2006: 40). These years eventually saw union membership experience its 'longest recorded decline', strike rates fall to 'lowest ever levels', collective bargaining arrangements shrink, and new human resource management practices emerge (Edwards et al. 1998: 1).

In this period, we can of course identify the emergence of some of the other features of a markedly changed labour market. The services sector grew both absolutely – after the economy pulled out of recession in the early 1980s – as well as relatively, although the 'new jobs' thus created were insufficient, in the context of growing labour market participation by women, to eliminate unemployment. Of these new jobs many, around half, were part-time, and thus failed to compensate on a one-to-one basis for the loss of mainly full-time jobs elsewhere. Employment in temporary jobs and self-employment also increased over this period: work became more 'precarious'. These changes were accompanied by a marked shift in the workforce gender balance.

Were we to stop at this point, the main thrust of our conclusion would be to note the very substantial weakening of the British trade union movement, distinguished by its close historical and institutional ties to the Labour party, extending to include funding, membership, and a role in policy formulation; to emphasize – like Glyn and Klein – the very active role played by the state, under Mrs Thatcher, in this process; and to note again that this weakening is widely viewed as being integral not only to the policy trajectories of the preceding governments of Thatcher and Major, but also to the context giving birth to the New Labour project and the policy platforms of the Blair governments. But the conflicts and transformations associated with Thatcherism did not emerge from a void, and while the significance of these 'shock' years for the trajectories thereafter of British capitalism, as well as for the emergence of the claims attaching to the New Labour project as a post-Thatcher modernizing force, is not to be doubted, some sense of prior economic contexts – and of their complexity – is equally important. In the next section, we confront one understanding of this prior context with another.

Shocks to the system: corporate destabilization as a prelude

In assessments today of the 'competitiveness' of the British economy, and certainly in much popular debate outside of some relatively specialized academic circles, it is nowadays regarded as an almost axiomatic thing that Britain before Thatcher suffered from overly strong trade unions and manifestly inefficient working practices. This in turn sustains a particular understanding in the United Kingdom today of what harsh economic realities require if the domestic economy is to be able to pay its way in the world – namely, weak trade unions, deregulated labour markets, and a permissive stance with regard to private capital. If we retain our concern in this chapter with the position of organized labour in Britain, a reasonable question to ask is how the evidence on this point looks, in retrospect. In asking this question, we also confront what might be called the *linear* interpretation of economic developments in the 1970s as a precursor to Thatcherism in the 1980s. In this view, increased international competition combined with trade union militancy to bring an end to the long boom that began with the reconstruction effort following the Second World War, and lasted through the 1950s and 1960s.

That this is a proposition worth considering is perhaps obvious. If the crisis of British capitalism in the 1970s simply reflected pressure on UK businesses from international competition (without) and trade unions (within), then dealing severely with trade unions might be defended not only as a rational choice for a government committed to the ideal of competition in the market place, but also a far easier target to aim at. Moreover, and while the politics of Andrew Glyn's assessments are not those of Mrs Thatcher, it is interesting to note a coincidence of views on this point. The pro-business defence of Thatcherism – necessary given the ineluctability of the market place – and a substantial body of left-wing commentary, including critics like Glyn (2006: 7), agree that the crisis for capitalism 'by the mid-1970s' was one of profits being squeezed by international competition on the one hand, and 'militant wage pressure' on the other. While a popular thesis, and not just for the United Kingdom, the evidence on this claim has been subjected to stringent criticism – the details of which we need not repeat at length here although the interested reader will get an idea of the issues from the chapter end notes.[4]

What we do now wish to show, by way of a brief pen sketch, is that a quite different take is possible on the crisis of British capitalism before Mrs Thatcher. This lends itself to a quite different interpretation of later economic and political developments, and points to a far more nuanced – and far more critical – understanding of Thatcherism. Most particularly, and as intimated in the chapter introduction, it allows us to deepen the terms of reference most usually brought to bear on the traumas of these years. The approach in question commences with a far more *active* understanding of what international competition means – one that recognizes the role of the state in forging the arenas within which firms compete, and the consequences of how firms actually do so. It is associated in the United Kingdom, most particularly, with the work of Keith Cowling.

Competitiveness and the transnational firm

Perhaps the quickest route to the point that we wish to make is to commence with the debate that began to gather pace in the United Kingdom from the 1970s, as perceptions grew that the manufacturing sectors upon which Britain depended for trade were struggling to maintain their competitive position in the wider world. In a much-cited passage from an influential study by the economist Ajit Singh, the problem was formulated thus. After first observing the historically specific structure of the UK economy vis-à-vis manufactured goods – 'a net importer of food and raw materials, which have to be paid for largely by exports of manufactures' – a potentially generalizable view of 'efficiency' for these key sectors followed: 'given the normal level of other components of the balance of payments, an efficient manufacturing industry is one which not only meets the needs of the consumers at the lowest cost, but also generates sufficient net exports to pay for the country's required level of imports at socially desired rates of employment, output growth, and exchange rate, both in the short and long runs' (Singh 1977).[5] The concern expressed by Singh and many others was that UK-based manufacturing was failing this test.

Over time, the significance of the Singh test has been expounded with great fluency. If firms based in an economy lose sales, whether in domestic markets to imports or in export markets abroad, and this leads to reserves of unused capacity vis-à-vis the production of goods and services, then for reasons that are self-evident productivity will suffer. Moreover, any attendant closure of plant or facility, or scrapping of capacity, could generate in turn not only higher levels of unemployment in those industries, but discourage the investment and innovation essential for future productivity growth. The outcome could be one of progressively worsening circumstances – here the works of Nicholas Kaldor and of processes of 'cumulative causation' are relevant – not only because of inhibited performance at the level of the firm, but also because of trade deficits and painful corrections at the macroeconomic level. This last point is of particular contextual importance to the UK debate in the 1970s, because governments then as previously were loathe to countenance currency devaluation as a means of correcting a trade deficit, fearing 'real wage resistance' and imported price inflation.[6]

But one limitation to this kind of approach is insufficient regard to the distinction which appears between corporate and national interests when firms can organize as cross-border producers. In the 1970s, following Britain's entry into the European Economic Community (EEC), a series of transnationally minded firms with operations in Britain – including American firms, some of which had entered the United Kingdom decades previously – moved decisively to develop the European theatre as an integrated base for their regional operations. As a result, important tranches of Britain's manufacturing economy were subjected to a destabilizing loss of jobs and output.

An apt example in this regard is the industry for car products and component parts. Here, ambitions for trade with the continental mainland very quickly came unstuck: a healthy trade surplus in cars at the start of the 1970s, just prior to EEC entry, turned to deficit by 1975 – and steadily worsened over the rest of the decade (see Wilks 1984: 70–5). And while it is true that the domestically owned segment of the UK-based industry failed to match a rising import penetration by European firms with offsetting exports, at a sectoral level the balance of trade between the United Kingdom and its EEC partners worsened far more dramatically and rapidly than this alone would have allowed. A major contributing factor was that US transnationals in Britain – Ford, General Motors (Vauxhall), and Chrysler (Talbot) – re-organized their regional operations to the detriment of Britain. So-called captive imports from the continental mainland to the United Kingdom organized by these firms grew sharply: Ford doubled up both as the dominant foreign car maker producing in Britain *and* Britain's biggest car importer (see ibid.: 71–2; Cowling 1982: 143). This large US impact on the car products side was matched by equally destabilizing manoeuvres by major British firms: companies like GKN, Lucas, and Associated Engineering, with a sizeable presence in car components as well as other manufacturing activities, expanded their interests in Europe. They did so partly by aggressive selling but also by acquiring mainland production facilities, pointing to further long-term difficulties vis-à-vis the balance of UK trade in these and other industries. Thus, when the automotive sector as a whole finally entered deficit in 1982, two main reasons – in addition to monetarism and Mrs Thatcher – were a now-persistent deficit in cars and a largely disappeared surplus in components (see Wilks, 1984: 71–2).

Fallouts and perceptions

The most immediate point which could be made here is simply to say that when firms are able to organize as transnational producers, a worsening performance in trade for a host economy need not reflect a loss of competitiveness for *these* firms. Their products may be just as desirable as before, their processes just as efficient; for that matter, their access to markets, or their cost positions, may well be improved. Other firms, those dependent on the business of firms (say) like Ford, or GKN, or Lucas, might of course suffer badly as a result, and with all the knock-on consequences outlined above. But if manufacturing in the United Kingdom in the 1970s was failing the 'Singh' test, this was at least partly because some individual businesses based in the United Kingdom were very actively seeking to enhance their positions in Europe, in the pursuit of privately approved gains.[7] And there is little evidence that they were driven to do so by UK trade unions: on a case by case basis, strategic rivalries with other corporations were a far more pressing issue.[8]

The next point is an important one. It is often suggested that entry to the EEC exposed a wholesale inefficiency in British manufacturing; with some leeway perhaps being allowed American operators like Ford, which while maintaining plants in the United Kingdom had nonetheless been scarcely disadvantaged by the experience. But in car components, largely in the hands of British firms, survey after survey in this period consistently pointed to cost and technical advantages *over* European rivals: 'UK component makers continue to be highly competitive' (Bhaskar 1979: 306). And insofar as these European rivals were concerned, British firms were *aggressive*: '[a]lthough European...companies have significant markets in the UK...British companies have been even more aggressive in their penetration of the European market' (ibid.: 305). The struggles of the car assembly section of the British-owned industry, in part explicable because British Leyland, unlike Ford and the big part suppliers, obtained no advantages from an expanded and integrated European base, has overshadowed an obvious fact.[9] But again, a distinction has to be made between a national benefit and a corporate interest: a significant part of corporate effort took the form of the development of facilities abroad – and the export of jobs.

But perhaps the most significant point is that this development may help explain a misconception that has never quite left the British popular conscience, which is that UK industry was somehow uniquely afflicted and affected in the 1970s by damaging industrial unrest. Contrary to this belief, the United Kingdom was actually a middle ranking country amongst the world's leading capitalist economies when it came to working days lost to strikes in this period. As data compiled by Glyn shows (2006: 32), over the period stretching from 1968 to 1979 the median number of strike days lost per 1000 workers, and in sectors defined principally for industrial workers, was higher in the United Kingdom than in a cluster of relatively low-strike countries in Europe – including the Scandinavian countries, Germany, and Holland – and even than in France, if 1968 is excluded. But the industrial relations situation was considerably 'worse' in Ireland, Spain, and Italy, and looking further abroad, worse too in the United States, Canada, and Australia. But unlike its major European counterparts, or for that matter North America or the Asia Pacific, UK-based manufacturing in this period saw a major co-incidental transfer of capacity overseas. The abiding refrain that Britain was rendered the 'sick man' of Europe, as a consequence of its over-mighty trade unions, may owe much to this phenomenon.

But if this is so, a different kind of political and economic history of this period is possible, one that takes us from the end of the post-war boom to Mrs Thatcher. The assumption that British firms had been rendered incompetent by militant trade unions demanding high wages at the expense of profits, and responsible for restrictive practices which had left a once-mighty manufacturing sector unable to compete, provided a key context against which the onslaught against British unions was later enacted. It is important not to oversimplify the range of factors at play in the 1970s: profound middle class fears – 'middle class' in the popular English sense – were engendered by the growing movement in the United Kingdom, as elsewhere, for industrial democracy, with little doubt that this was interpreted as an encroachment on managerial prerogatives; economic downturn; public dissatisfaction or unease over industrial unrest; and ongoing price inflation – the latter given a hefty push by commodity and oil prices – were real factors. These fears and stresses are brilliantly captured by Glyn (2006: 1–23): but these, it should be remembered, and as Glyn emphasizes, were equally live issues elsewhere.

Insofar as how one goes about sketching an alternative perspective on what was to emerge from this febrile period later, we could ask how the specific sense that UK-based manufacturing was wilting against Europe played upon developing political contexts, as a force helping shape and forge public opinion. Again, one must not oversimplify: the difficulties experienced by Labour government incomes policy before Mrs Thatcher, although broadly successful, or the rising unemployment of the later 1970s as the same Labour government opted for austerity measures, all these and more would be factors on the 'economic side' of the equation to consider. Equally, highlighting the destabilizing consequences of corporate activity in the 1970s, as a subtext to the problems of de-industrialization increasingly identified for Britain, is in no way to suggest that the blow later delivered by monetarism was not substantial. The 1981–1982 recession delivered a loss of something in the region of between one-fifth and one-sixth of manufacturing capacity. But it would be hard to account for the UK's willingness to sacrifice swathes of British industry to accommodate the effects of EEC entry in the 1970s were it not the case that for many large producers – including the US giants – Europe, rather than the United Kingdom, was already the strategic theatre of operations. And similarly, it is germane to speculate on the unforeseen political advantages which EEC entry gave the developing movement later christened Thatcherism vis-à-vis its growing attack on organized labour.

Reflections and accommodations: competitiveness in a porous economy

One of the most fascinating, if complex, issues raised by the varieties of capitalism debate is the persistence over time of meaningful differences in economic organization within nation states, each readily characterized as capitalist, within the framework of a wider global economy. The practical importance of maintaining a grasp of each level of analysis is obvious when considering the contexts and impacts of the 'shock' years of 1980s Britain – self-evidently possessing features distinct and specific to the United Kingdom, but at the same time susceptible only to a partial assessment without the benefit of a broader purview. The details, however organized and appraised, confirm a quite general point made by David Coates (see Coates 2005a: 270–1), regarding the importance of historically minded and globally aware assessments of national economic trajectories. But they also provide a context within which to locate today's policy consensus, amongst the leadership of Britain's main political parties, favouring a 'porous' real economy with minimum frictions – and, in particular, 'onerous' employment rights – to deter favourable decisions by transnational firms seeking a location for investment.

It may be a moot point whether it is possible at this juncture to separate the two defining parts of this proposition, which is that Britain's economy is dependent on the favourable investment decisions of transnational firms, and that this in turn requires deregulated labour markets so that the United Kingdom will be an attractive venue for them. Following on from the 'hollowing out' experienced by tracts of the UK industrial economy before Mrs Thatcher's election, but grossly exacerbated thereafter in her first years in office, a growing emphasis became discernible on the 'new' attractiveness of Britain not just to investment but to *foreign* inward direct investment, and with regard not only to the principal historic source of this kind of injection (the US) but increasingly also from Japan – giving rise to the 'Japanization' mania of the 1980s and beyond. This is consistent with the dawning realization of a decapitated industrial economy; and it provides one important inherited context for the first New Labour government.

But at the same time that there is little doubt but that Mrs Thatcher was sincere in her despise of organized labour, one would hesitate to doubt the sincerity with which the policy attitudes of New Labour with respect to employment rights for workers in the United Kingdom have been struck vis-à-vis the perceived interests of business. As Tony Blair put it shortly after his election as prime minister, Britain would maintain 'the most lightly regulated labour market of any leading economy in the world' (from Tony Blair's foreword to the 1998 White Paper *Fairness at Work*, cited Coates 2005c: 85). As David Coates notes, while some small nods were made in the direction of Labour's trade union supporters from the point it entered government – on union membership rights, on some individual rights at work, on parental and maternity leave – the general determination was to 'minimise the impact on business'. The zeal with which attempts from within the EU to strengthen workers' rights were resisted, both as these affected Britain but also in Europe more generally, was notable (see Coates ibid.: 81–7). If conceding the internal political space on workers rights to business, and if acting as a conduit for the interests of regionally focused businesses in Europe, it could hardly be doubted that New Labour embraced its inheritance.

Thus if we are looking to understand today's policy consensus, we have what may well be a deeply felt recognition of the internationalization of Britain's industrial base, framed by a regard conditioned less by proven long-term benefits than by an historically conditioned reflex to straitened circumstances now transcending normal standards of rational inspection or party political allegiances. But we may also have the winning impact of a sustained ideological assault – Mrs Thatcher's victory.

It is interesting to note that a recent study of the United Kingdom in the 1990s of branch closure decisions by multiple plant firms found that sites with a strong union presence were the ones most likely to be closed down (see Addison et al. 2003) – a finding which highlights the limited value of the early promise of New Labour that workers should have 'rights against discrimination for making a free choice of being a union member' (again from Tony Blair's foreword to *Fairness at Work*; cited Coates 2005c: 84). It is precisely this sort of conduct by firms which weak employment legislation allows. And against this kind of capability, possessed by many large concerns, the difficulties posed for organized labour when production crosses borders are profound.[10] But the presumption that labour market deregulation is prerequisite to national economic competitiveness goes further in its effects than just the position of those workers employed in the transnationally organized production of traded goods and services. The onslaught against organized labour in the Thatcher period has not been repeated, but neither can it be said that it has in any sense been repealed.

In all of this it would be quite misleading to see the UK economy as a passive victim of a globalization process, since globalization, in most of the senses in which this word is nowadays used, is not something that has simply happened *to* Britain, if by this we mean that its economy has been subjected to pressures in the development of which its state has played no part, and regarding which it has had no resources but to accommodate. Britain was, of course, initially excluded from joining the original EEC, established in 1958 via the Treaty of Rome to build on earlier economic cooperation between its founding members, for reasons including (amongst other things) its substantial interests in the British Commonwealth – evolved from the ashes of the old Empire. And British entry, when it occurred some fifteen years later (in 1973) with considerable domestic acrimony from both the political left and right, took place because of the strong, active, and combined support of senior political figures in each of the main political parties. Strong industrial and commercial interests, including those large transnational manufacturing firms noted in an earlier section, lobbied strongly in favour of this outcome, indigenous concerns as well as American. But our point here is not that there is a debate over whether entry was right or wrong, or that more work is needed on the question as to why Britain should have proved so vulnerable in this period to the regionalizing activities of some of its largest firms, but that at every stage of development there was very little that was passive about it.[11]

The same, of course, could be said about other features of the internationalization of the ownership of swathes of the UK economy. Although we should again take care not to lose sight of the fact that British firms are also major overseas investors, it is hard not to be impressed by the successive intrusion of foreign direct investment into areas quite distinct from the UK manufacturing and industrial sectors: in the utilities; in services; in banking and finance; even in the City itself – which rapidly succumbed to entry by foreign players following deregulation (the 'Big Bang') in the 1980s. These developments have no doubt helped recent entrenched policy attitudes.

Post-Fordism as a literary phenomenon: an interpretation

In this last section, we turn to briefly consider the argument that the retarded economic performance experienced in Western capitalism in the 1970s reflected the exhaustion of a distinctively Fordist system of mass production. The literary output, of the past twenty or so years, on this theme, has been immense: in his important study of comparative models of capitalism, Coates (2000) rightly draws attention to the proliferation of analyses – from the 1980s – which sought to explain the end of the post-Second World War boom by reference to a transitionary progression from a Fordist to a post-Fordist state. Referring to the US 'social systems of accumulation' and Euro-led 'regulation' schools, and also to works inspired by Piore and Sabel's (1984) thesis of a new 'industrial divide' in the Western economic order, Coates notes how 'time and again' the argument advanced was that the 'postwar golden age had been organized on the basis of Fordist mass production', but 'was now shifting to a new paradigm of organization variously labelled "flexible specialisation", the "new competition", "disorganized capitalism", "reflexive accumulation", or "post-Fordism"' (Coates 2000: 42). While a full assessment of this literature lies well beyond the scope of this book, we can nonetheless highlight some particularly prominent features, and offer some comments accordingly.

As normally employed, the term Fordist mass production implies some notion of a definite type of large-scale factory system, predicated on scale economies in production, said to have become dominant in post-Second World War America, and responsible for its economic advantages over only partly assimilated Western European economies. The privilege thereby accorded the Ford family name in this literature is no doubt double edged: under Henry Ford, the US motor company is held to have first perfected and then bequeathed a system of production capable of raising secular standards of living for working populations, but notable for its deleterious effects on the quality of working life and for the limited choices offered workers in their dual roles as consumers. Readers are often reminded *inter alia* of the five dollar day – and of Henry Ford's proclamation that suitably remunerated masses were needed who could afford to buy the goods they were employed to produce; of the iconic images of serially arranged equipment and processes staffed by ranks of serially arranged workers tasked with performing discrete and repetitive operations; and of the original Ford Model T motor car, available, as per the cliché, in all colours 'black'. As an additional feature, reference is also often made to the degree of control maintained by organizing firms over the span of relevant operations via vertical integration – with the Ford River Rouge complex in 1920s Detroit sometimes offered as an extreme instance.

Given this, one prominent trick in post-Fordist writing is to use the various parts of this construction to show – via simple inversion – how the world has changed. For example, consumers purchasing the early Ford Model T allegedly had little choice as regards not only colour but also features of the model; but by contrast, consumers in the post-Fordist world have far more scope for choice and selection – the key point from the viewpoint of this thesis being that this only became true somewhere in the 1970s. 'Fordist practices came to be seen as limiting', according to Anthony Giddens in a recent edition of *Sociology*, 'because they were suited to the manufacture of large quantities of standardized goods... [but] shifts were occurring in global consumerism, [and] the mass markets which had made Fordism so successful were being supplanted by "niche markets"'; thus the 'golden age' of the post-Second World War boom ended, giving way from Fordism to a 'new era of capitalist economic production', of 'flexibility and innovation', and of 'customised' goods (Giddens 2001: 384, 386).

We can immediately observe here that a strong feature of this kind of prospectus – one running right through many of the contributions noted by Coates – is that the transition from Fordism placed consumers on an improved footing vis-à-vis the firm. Next we can note that the principal example used for illustration is historical nonsense. Contrary to what one would imagine from an exposure to 'post-Fordism', the golden age of the post-Second World War boom saw the emergence of an extensive body of descriptive writing – both from factory visitors and contemporary academic writers – hailing the flexibility of '1950s' manufacturing processes, and 'customization'. A larger sample of instances is given in Coffey (2006: 15–43), building on Lyddon (1996), but to take one example, a US industry historian writing in the mid-1960s about car factory achievements in the mid-1950s described how 'preferences would roll off the assembly line in company with others representing different assortment of choices', after glowing over choices for 'engines, body styles, colors for both exterior and interior, and even hubcaps... radio, heater, air-conditioning' – with 'assembly of motor vehicles' coming 'a long way since Henry Ford's pioneering days' (see Rae 1965: 200). What do we make of this?

One way of approaching this question, albeit perhaps not the easiest one for contributors to the post-Fordist cannon, is to reconsider the sub-texts of the thesis, commencing with the 'received understanding' of a system of Fordist mass production. We might treat this as a fabricated narrative assembled from partly imaginary materials – projected onto the past as a retrospective historical fiction in order to legitimate the present. For example, in the decades after the Second World War, and in addition to materials praising the ingenuity of corporations in expanding choice and variety for consumers, a parallel body of critical literature also emerged, focusing on the roles of horizontal and vertical product differentiation – realized via flexible assembly systems and of regular styling changes over time – in consolidating the grip of a small number of giant firms on increasingly oligopolistic industrial structures (see Coffey 2006: 35–8). For some critics at least, these developments in 'flexibility and innovation' were at the consumer's expense. While just one example, from it we can see how a counterfactual history for a manufacturing industry comes with an accompanying narrowing of precepts vis-à-vis consumer sovereignty, and lacking critical counterpoint.

In addition to the distortions of fictionalized history and an unacknowledged shifting in precepts and assumptions, there is also the 'Orientalism' to consider. For example, it is almost a *leitmotif* of the Anglo-American strains of post-Fordism that in the auto industry 'flexibility' and 'customization' came from Japan in the 1970s. Toyota, in particular, is heralded in each of these studies because – again Giddens (2001) – it was able to offer '[c]hanges in designs, options and features' (ibid.: 385). But it is simply untrue that the industry which made Ford a household name was unable to manage changes to 'options', 'designs', or 'features' until taught to do so in the 1970s. And while there is perhaps a little more to this kind of 'Othering', identified by some political theorists in the changing forms of Western trade debates vis-à-vis Japan, a marked feature of the post-Fordist literature has been use of freely invented and demonstrably inaccurate Japanese examples to re-imagine the Western industrial past.[12]

A complex instance of this can be identified in the claim that the 'Japanization' of production – a hugely popular theme ten to fifteen years ago – would entail the development of more vertically de-integrated production structures; on grounds that this is what successful, flexible and radically different firms like Toyota did. From sometime around the middle part of the 1980s and into the 1990s it became *de rigueur* in management and social science literatures dealing with Japan vis-à-vis the West to emphasize that the Japanese firm was a 'vertically de-integrated entity' (Ruigrock and

Van Tulder 1995: 39; also 51–4; also cited in Coffey and Tomlinson 2003: 124). But for the auto industry, where this kind of claim was to be repeatedly made, the evidence is in fact a great deal more complex than this. Moreover, if one steps back a little further – to the later 1970s or early 1980s – something quite different was being said: commentators would tend to emphasize how vertically integrated leading Japanese car makers like Toyota or Nissan were compared to Western firms. The change in the interim in no way reflects a change in the balance of carefully observed evidence: the assertion simply appears, and then spreads (see Coffey 2006: 165–168).[13] If one then considers why this might have happened, 'domestic' developments in the West may be an appropriate starting point: by the middle 1980s in the United States, the wholesale shifting by indigenous manufacturers from larger unionized to smaller de-unionized sites, was already well under way – with similar, if less pronounced, trends in Europe. Or, more abstractedly, consider the new sense that 'planning' of any sort – including 'vertical control' – was defunct.

The point perhaps becomes sharpest when considering more generally the associations drawn in the post-Fordist stream between work and consumption. Although the functionalities are never quite explained, it is frequently asserted that new skills and working practices associated with the end of Fordism, as a corollary to now more flexible production processes with enhanced customer choice at the end (processes associated according to some texts with 'high' rather than 'low' trust employment) have at the same time occurred in such a way that the role of trade unions disappears. And again, it is hard not to see a legitimating principle at play with reference to the works of modernity.

Some contributors adopting a 'break with Fordism' perspective are more critical, and portray to a larger extent than this implies the presence of active strategies of union avoidance or union busting on the part of the corporate sector. It is interesting in this connection to note the emergence of works like Buechler (2000), who sees the 'transition to post-Fordism' as undermining 'traditional bases of mobilization', making social activism outside of traditional labour movement structures more likely. But what insight the categories 'Fordism' and 'post-Fordism' provide is not clear, if stripped of the counterfactual assumptions and contrasts which usually accompany. Simply to say that the first describes the world 'as it was', and the second 'as it is' adds little. It may be that even in critical writing a principle role is to stand in lieu of evidence. For example, the use of these categories to explain the end of the post-Second World War boom, whether in the United Kingdom or United States or elsewhere, are never, upon inspection, very convincing.[14]

As a positive explanation of a period of trauma and crisis, post-Fordist literature possesses little of empirical appeal: but it may be that in the longer term, its most lasting contribution will be less its explanatory value and more its oddly reflective character, not as an explanation of the 'shock' years of the 1980s, but as one intellectual response.

Summing up

The point of departure in this chapter is a shared premise in each of several recent contributions to the debate on worldwide capitalist trajectories, emphasizing the radicalism of the ruptures of the 1980s vis-à-vis phenomenon like Thatcherism with the seemingly stable social settlements in Western and other economies that appeared to emerge during the preceding period of sustained growth. This has been characterized (or caricatured) as the post-Second World War 'golden age' lasting through to the late 1960s, and ending painfully in the 1970s, a period of economic and social tension. In the particular case of the United Kingdom, this difficult decade was followed by the 'shock' of massive jobs losses and destruction of industrial capacity in traditional union strongholds; with the gradual acclimatization of British public opinion to mass (male) unemployment; and with a new emphasis on labour market deregulation and weak unions as a necessary condition for competitiveness of the national economy in a harsher international climate. In this connection, a widely agreed view of what happened holds that a strong labour movement in the post-war era sowed the seeds of its own demise at this later juncture – that trade union militancy combined with international competition to create a crisis for British capitalism, the context in turn within which later developments must be placed.

Against this, we propose that a less linear assessment of developing economic and political trajectories in the 1970s permits a more nuanced assessment of the later course of the onslaught against organized labour. While accepting that the United Kingdom in the 1980s saw radical departures in state economic policy, we consider how attention to the destabilizing consequences of the regional activities of profit-seeking firms in the previous decade might facilitate an understanding of Thatcherism that gives more scope to its opportunistic nature and is less fatalistic in its assessments. This allows a more subtle context in which to understand the 'shocks' of the 1980s; and it highlights the role of intellectual as well as practical conversion in explaining the willingness of proponents of the New Labour project in the 1990s and beyond to endorse aspects of the Thatcher revolution as not only retrospectively welcome, but also necessary.

3
The Commanding State: The Politics of Competitiveness

The question as to whether (and how) to regulate the activities of firms which operate across the borders of nation states is, not surprisingly, a deeply controversial one. In the course of the preceding chapter, we observed the role played by the regional operations of US firms like Ford Motors as well as large British firms in destabilizing the British manufacturing economy in the 1970s vis-à-vis Europe; and also some wider ranging significances of this, as a catalyzing factor in the subsequent onslaughts against Britain's trade unions, and as a context for later competitiveness debates. We noted too that one of the more obvious concessions in New Labour policy thinking to previous policy trajectories has been to accept, endorse, and even promote the sort of deregulatory measures which its Conservative party predecessors deemed to be a mainstay of industrial policy, to attract and retain investment by firms. On this issue, a definite stance has been adopted and despite the traumas currently being experienced as a consequence of the still unfolding international banking and credit crisis it is far from obvious that this in and of itself will lead to any sort of major policy rethinking among the leadership of the United Kingdom's main political parties as to the desirability of pursuing competitiveness by courting investment from transnational corporate players via deregulation and easy terms of entry and exit. In this chapter, we confront some implications of this now deeply embedded policy stance by considering the manner in which the state responds to a public policy embarrassment. We choose for this purpose the circumstances of the decision of Ford Motors – in 2000 – to fully withdraw Ford-badged cars from UK assembly.

The selection of this case is not an incidental one. The automotive industry remains a flagship sector for British industrial policy as this pertains to manufacture, and manufacturing activity as a whole still accounts, despite its declining share in domestic production, for the larger part of Britain's trade with the rest of the world. Moreover, the Ford announcement came just three years into the first Blair government, elected with a commanding majority, and still enjoying the degrees of freedom and public support awarded by the afterglow – able, if so desiring, to make a mark by its response. The prominence attaching to the case guaranteed both public exposure and a parliamentary investigation, empowered by law to take evidence on the circumstances attending the event and to report on these and on the adequacy of government policy. From the viewpoint of further identifying the 'character' of New Labour in early office, and with particular regard to issues of continuity and change in relation to predecessors, both the timing and prominence of the Ford case are significant framing features. In addition, the involvement of a parliamentary investigation, with a cross-party composition and submissions taken from the relevant government department, opens other windows.

As we will see, in the course of accounting for their actions Ford's executives advanced a defence which casts novel light on the strategic positioning of this large American firm in its European theatre of operations, and presents an illuminating example of the workaday question as to how large transnational producers exert bargaining leverages – how they organize and exploit 'reach'. Here Glyn's (2006: 101) observation that threats of industrial relocation, even if 'only exercised periodically', are an important lever to be occasionally pulled by transnationally organized producers, is apt.[1] A charge was mounted by the trade unions representing the workers whose jobs were lost as a result of Ford's decision that the closure was a *punishment* exercise mounted in response to workplace disputes at the affected plant – bringing us to consider one of the harsher implications of New Labour's proclaimed views on labour legislation. Moreover, the details of this case carry us beyond issues of class and union organization to questions of race, because prior to the surprise announcement that UK-based assembly of Ford cars would cease, a high-profile union campaign against shop-floor racism at the very factory complex hit by the closure decision had gained much press coverage. And when the hammer blow fell, it fell most heavily on the Asian sections of the workforce.

Our principal motivation in all of this is with what we can learn about the contemporary character of British capitalism today. As the intricacies of this complex but highly revealing case are layered back, we ask whether, and via a parsing of the circumstances of this specific and discrete event – a factory closure announced without prior warning by a major transnational producer – not only the organs of government policy administration but also of scrutiny of policy by Parliament stand revealed as capable or incapable of mapping the industrial realities of Britain today; and of offering, where appropriate, substantive criticism of policy trajectories. Our closing contribution in this regard makes use of the flagship status accorded the car sector in government policies towards manufacturing more generally to further some of the preliminary comments offered in the preceding chapter about the UK competitiveness debate; here we touch, in a revealing way, on the topic of 'lean production'.

The event and the investigation

It seems obvious enough that Ford, from a British perspective, is a foreign-owned transnational, carrying a family name as American as apple pie. But there is little doubt that the sheer longevity of Ford's presence added much to the surprise caused by its decision to withdraw from UK-based car assembly, at least in the near term. In the previous chapter we used the example of the car industry to illustrate the important role played by the positioning of transnational corporations in the 1970s, British as well as foreign owned, in exacerbating difficulties in the UK economy. If Ford's early entry as a major foreign direct investor in car and truck manufacture contributed positively to the comparative breadth and strength of UK-based manufacturing activity for many decades, its later repositioning illustrates, in this connection, the vulnerability of national economies to the decisions of transnational firms to rebalance operations. In this respect, it is fitting that Ford provide the subject for our case study, which again deals with questions of capacity, location, and sales. It is perhaps as well to commence with the biographical details of the company's announcement that it would cease car assembly in Britain, which can be stated quite easily, at least in outline.

At the point when Ford made its announcement cars carrying the Ford badge were still being assembled at one site only in the United Kingdom, at the Ford Dagenham complex, a site based near London, and adjacent to the River Thames. Several years earlier, the company had elected to withdraw Ford cars from its other site at Halewood (near Liverpool). When the Dagenham site was founded – Edsel Ford cut the first sod in 1929 – it had been the largest car factory in Europe; and while Ford manufacturing activities in the United Kingdom pre-date this, with imported parts previously assembled elsewhere, it is really with the founding of this complex that the era of Ford volume operations in Britain commenced in earnest.[2] The announcement that car assembly operations would cease came on 12 May 2000, ending almost 70 years of continuous production. At this juncture, as well as being the only plant to assemble Ford cars in the United Kingdom, Dagenham was building cars sourced only from a single model-range, the Ford Fiesta: Ford announced that when the model terminated (in 2002), it would not be replaced by a UK-assembled car. Ford did, how-ever, announce that operations would continue at the diesel engine plant also sited at Dagenham, with some expansion in capacity, out-put, and range, and a limited reassignment of workers. Ford's with-drawal was thus not 'complete', but the better part of some 3000 directly affected assembly plant jobs at Dagenham were lost, while the decision had significant consequences for UK-based supply chains.

The publicity generated by the decision would in all likelihood have made some form of parliamentary investigation inevitable, but by an unhappy coincidence for the British government equally unwelcome decisions were taken in that same year by some of the other major for-eign players in the UK car sector: the German firm BMW announced that it would break up the Rover Group, and General Motors (Vauxhall) announced that it would cease car assembly operations at its (British) Luton site.[3] With the government placed, for a brief time at least, under some public pressure to respond, the House of Commons Trade and Industry Committee – a cross-party parliamentary body charged with scrutinizing government policies and empowered to require sub-mission from involved parties of written evidence and documents and to take oral testimony from witnesses, on the basis of public question-answer sessions – held an inquiry, publishing its findings in a report (hereafter HC 2000–2001) intended to inform parliamentary debate. We use this inquiry, and focusing on the circumstances of the Ford closure for reasons to which we will return in a later section of this chapter, as a means by which to enter into the case.

Rather than commence with a full account of testimonies to the parliamentary committee and with the main body of the committee's report, it will be easiest in this instance to move directly to some main points of interest, establishing themes and points of analysis in a simple way – with due attention to cross connections – before expanding outwards to consider further the broader narrative forms of testimony and report, their texts and subtexts. Again, the selected points are easily sketched in outline.

In the course of responding to a series of questions put to them publicly by the Members of Parliament making up the Trade and Industry Committee, the Ford executives attending the hearing gave negative answers to each of two queries (both of some importance, and both to be considered in more detail in the fourth section, below). Asked if car assembly operations were to cease at Ford Dagenham because (a) of Britain's failure to enter the Euro zone and (b) of the light protections afforded British workers, in both instances the Ford Motor Company response was firmly in the negative.

Instead, when pressed as to why car assembly operations had been withdrawn from the United Kingdom, assurances were offered that the Dagenham closure was a reflection of concerns that were Europe-wide, rather than specific to the United Kingdom. Ford, as represented in the person of the chairman and managing director of Ford Motor Company Ltd., pointed towards resource-pooling and capacity consolidation, as a Europe-wide phenomenon:

> [T]he industry worldwide and also in Europe is suffering from overcapacity... running plants at less than full capacity incurs additional fixed costs and the whole impact of that has resulted in very poor financial returns... rationalization has been occurring. (HC 2000–2001: 1)

The explanation offered was thus that global demand was insufficiently buoyant to justify maintaining the existing number of factory sites for Ford operations in Europe: some rationalization was needed to reduce fixed costs via consolidation.

This did not mean, however, that Ford had no intention of proceeding with a successor to the Ford Fiesta: rather, assembly operations for the new car would be relocated from Britain to Germany, to Cologne. And in a rather complex arrangement, another plant at Valencia in Spain would provide some additional production of the new car to supplement the facility at Cologne – Valencia would assemble this new car alongside its existing operations on another model.[4] In this way, while several sites (Cologne and Valencia) would be involved in building the new car which would replace the older Ford Fiesta assembled at Dagenham, the overall number of factories maintained by Ford in Europe for car assembly would be reduced. And in an interesting twist to the defence, Ford's witnesses supplied a supplementary explanation of why one of the three sites involved should close (Dagenham) while another (Valencia) should 'double up':

> [W]e decided that the most appropriate way to run assembly operations was not to dedicate one particular plant to one particular car but to have more flexible operations. The technical term is *swing plant*, which means that you can change production of a model which may be falling in demand into one which is increasing in demand. (HC 2000–2001: 6; emphasis added)

The Valencia site in Spain would double up as a 'swing plant' supporting Cologne by backing-up its production for the replacement to the old Fiesta, thereby producing an outcome with a reduced number of sites overall, and with the United Kingdom losing out.

When pressed further as to why a 'rationalization' of capacity should mean the specific choice of Dagenham as *the* site which would lose out in the Ford network, assurances were again offered that there was little specifically *wrong* with the UK site:

> the balance of operations was that Dagenham did not have an offsetting advantage which would suggest we should close another plant. That was essentially it. (HC 2000–2001:6)

In other words, the Dagenham site lost out as the result of a simple process of default.

Upon being pressed on whether relations with the workforce were at issue some concession to this view was hinted at, but then sidelined as a minor point. In the oral evidence given before the

Trade and Industry Committee, it was revealed that managers at the Dagenham site had complained of problems with the state of 'cooperation', 'culture change', and 'competitive performance' at the plant, and that the unions' representative had charged the company with closing the plant as a consequence of a running dispute over new working practices at the site. Ford categorically denied, however, that poor workplace relations played a determining role in their decision. That the announcement overturned earlier, but quite recent and very explicit, assurances on the future of the plant given to the Dagenham workforce was brushed aside.

Swing plants and punishments

These then were the principal responses of the Ford Motor Company to the parliamentary committee, and in the next section we will consider how the committee responded. But before doing so, and as a preparatory exercise, we first pause to ask what could reasonably be made of the Ford testimony – *taken on its own terms* – and how it then looks if interpreted in the light of the charge levelled against it by the unions representing workers who lost their jobs as a consequence of the factory closure decision. We do so in order to be able to contrast our own assessment with that of the committee.

We should first observe again some immediately salient features of the case:

1. The cessation of car assembly operations at the Ford Dagenham site was abrupt, although from a company viewpoint operations were relocated rather than terminated; the afflicted parties were Ford workers in Britain and the UK industrial base.
2. An explanation was initially offered by Ford executives linking the closure decision to a potential shortfall in demand that vitiated previous investment plans; this was then supplemented with an economizing argument mounted on the idea of reducing the number of sites by developing so-called 'swing plants' for assembly work – better able to withstand changes in demand via a switch of resources between product lines.
3. A charge was mounted by Ford workers via their union representatives that the decision to cease car assembly operations at Dagenham was a 'punishment'.

Our principal question in the first instance might be to ask under what conditions an anticipated shortfall in (global) demand vis-à-vis capacity could reasonably be expected to reduce the number of car assembly sites employed by Ford to produce an unchanged number of product lines, *at the expense of one of its sites*. From here we are then in a position to consider the counter-claim made by the workers, and in this connection we also assess the particular claims made on behalf of 'swing plants' by the company.

To explore these issues all that we really need by way of an expository tool is a scale curve showing how car assembly costs might vary with projected output. Let us suppose initially that relevant costs are the *fixed costs* of a plant – onsite overhead plus the fixed costs of facility, equipment, and tooling – and the *wage costs* of assembly. We will assume that the wage costs of each car built are relatively stable vis-à-vis changes in scale of production, at least over the range of outputs with which we are concerned; if this is so, then because fixed costs (including onsite overheads) will spread over a progressively larger number of units of output as production expands, the overall average cost of assembling a car will fall as the scale of activity increases.[5]

Given this kind of cost projection we can see that Ford managers could reasonably argue that at any given site average costs would be higher the further factory demand fell below capacity, and for reasons to do with the role played by fixed costs relative to output. At the same time, however, because the crux of Ford's argument was that a shortfall in (global) demand required that it consolidate production at a reduced number of factory sites, we need to adapt the simple scale curve tool so that it can be used to compare aggregates, each comprised of production distributed over a different number of separate factory sites. For this reason, we will add the following assumption: *once* the number of factory sites is determined the *wage* cost of assembling a car – any car – is the same at all sites. This allows us to employ aggregate scale curves to compare *groups* of factory sites.[6]

To see how these can be used to investigate the internal logic of the Ford testimony as an explanation of events, we could proceed as follows. The scenario is one in which reducing the number of factory sites is argued by a firm (Ford) to make economic sense once production overall falls *below* a critical rate, Q^*. This could be interpreted as being analogous to a situation in which a projected aggregate scale curve for production involving fewer sites cuts a projected aggregate scale curve for production with more sites at just this point; and in such a way that at lower rates of activity operating with fewer sites becomes cheaper. We show this in Figure 3.1. If curve XX represents a scale curve with fewer sites, and YY a scale curve with more, then we have a scenario consistent with the Ford evidence: they intersect at point Q*, and for outputs below this point the scale curve with fewer sites (XX) represents lower production cost. But this begs the question: why *should* projected scale curves intersect in this fashion?

The answer to this question is subtle. Ford's testimony put great weight on the need to reduce fixed costs by consolidating production at fewer car assembly sites; and it seems intuitive enough that savings *could* be made here, because even with similar choices on equipment and tooling, savings could be realized on overheads and facility. This in turn would be enough to explain the relative slopes of curves XX and YY. The first curve would be flatter because with a smaller aggregated fixed cost, average costs overall are less sensitive to any reduction in the scale of activity. With the scale sensitive part of cost – the fixed cost – less significant, average cost would rise less sharply.

However, it would still fail to explain why the two curves should intersect. If the only difference were that fixed costs for a firm like Ford are lower in the aggregate when fewer production sites are employed, then fewer sites would always be cheaper. The decision

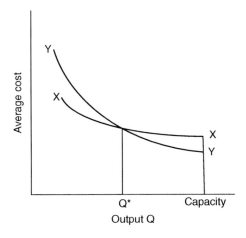

Figure 3.1   Intersecting aggregate scale curves

would not be contingent upon whether or not global demand projections fall below some critical rate of production, like the rate Q^* in Figure 3.1. There must therefore be *another* dimension of cost to consider: for example, wage cost.[7]

We have assumed for purposes of our simple expository diagram that once the number of factory sites at which a firm produces is determined then the wage cost of each product made is more or less the same at each site. This does not mean, however, that the level at which this wage cost settles cannot be affected by the number of factory sites which the firm in question elects to employ for production. And were we to now assume that the wage cost level is expected to be lower with more sites, and higher with fewer sites, we would have a situation analogous to that in Figure 3.1, where the scale curves cross. At lower rates of activity – below Q^* – running with fewer sites is preferred, because at these reduced outputs the pressure to economize on fixed cost is paramount; but at higher rates, it would be safe to run with more sites to exploit wage cost advantages.

If we ask the question 'how likely is this', it is perhaps worth observing that this is precisely the assumption running through case studies and other forms of empirical study that estimate the advantages of transnational producers at the bargaining table with workers on questions of wage cost – as already discussed in this book.[8] If wage rates are held to lower levels, or work intensities maintained at a higher pitch, or both, because maintaining a larger rather than a small number of production sites enhances the bargaining power of the firm, then this is consistent with the above scenario.

But if the only reason for a firm like Ford to maintain multiple sites in different countries – other than its ability to bargain hard with suppliers, or distributors, or national governments – is because advantages exist which outweigh added fixed costs, we can then see a possible *reconciliation* between Ford's evidence to the parliamentary committee investigating the loss of the Dagenham car assembly plant, and the trade union complaint to that committee that the closure was a punishment. In the first instance, if a company fails to believe that there *is* a wage cost advantage from maintaining more rather than fewer sites, consolidation may follow. In the second, a strategically minded firm would always be sensitive to the possibility that a failure to get its way with employees at one site might set a bad example for employees at others – here the occasional 'execution'

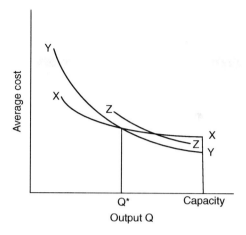

Figure 3.2   Scale curves and swing plant advantages

of a closure may again be a reasoned consideration. In any case, the two categories of explanation are *not* mutually exclusive: a reduced demand forecast could account for the loss of a site within a group of sites; and workplace tensions at any individual site could also occasion a particular closure decision.

One last complication remains, however, namely Ford's specific claim in evidence to the parliamentary committee on the benefits of 'swing plants' – factories which by housing production of adjacent car lines permit workers to be moved from products where demand is falling to products where demand is rising. While there is nothing objectionable per se in the reasoning here as far as it goes, a moment's thought suffices to establish that this seeming complication barely changes the above analysis. If workers are easily transferred across car lines within a large factory complex, and assuming of course that the costs of hiring or firing are positive, there could indeed be an advantage to running with several adjacent car lines at a single plant location.[9] But while true, the only effect of this would be to change the critical rate of production activity below which fewer rather than more plant sites is cost effective: to each aggregate scale curve would be added a further cost allowance when comparing projected costs – and the larger cost allowance would be added in the scenario with more rather than fewer sites. Developing our previous figure, we can see that little changes. In terms of Figure 3.2, we can think of an extra cost allowance shifting curve YY to position ZZ, say; and perhaps a similar shift in the other cost curve, but to a smaller degree (not drawn). But the only net effect would be to change the *position* of the critical rate of production at which the cost curves intersect (this would now lie to the right of Q^*). But insofar as the basic terms of our assessment in this section are concerned, nothing of principle would alter.

Were we to summarize at this juncture, the key point would be that in response to the promptings of a parliamentary committee, investigating a controversial and unexpected plant closure decision, Ford supplied a 'market exigencies' defence, in a context where complaints had been received from the worker side of a punitive measure, part of which concerned claims of disputations over working practices at the site. On inspection, these seemingly contrary claims are potentially consistent, even reinforcing; a reduced demand projection, or rising workplace tensions, would act in the same way, and in the context of a 'bargaining game' structured by both kinds of consideration. On this last point, the logic of Ford's own evidence concedes ground – tacitly, because the point has to be teased out through considered analysis – on employment issues. And here nothing of substance alters with the 'technocratic' twist added by Ford on 'swing plants'. Let us now consider, against this, what the committee did with this testimony.

Questions not asked and answers not given

With these preliminary facts and key points of evidence, and our own preliminary views in place to compare with, we now come to how the parliamentary committee responded. There is not space to convey more than a brief sense of the initial proceedings. The Committee was dazzled with the 'facts' of globalization – Ford's witnesses regaled it with a litany of mergers, acquisitions, and collaborative ventures as evidence of sweeping programmes of 'consolidation' in the industry: 'Daimler and Chrysler... Renault... with Nissan, VW taking over both Seat, Skoda and of course Bentley, GM took over Saab... an arrangement with Fiat'; and so forth (HC 2000–2001: 1). The Committee was properly reminded of Ford's other businesses in the United Kingdom: '[w]e bought Aston Martin about ten years ago, we bought Jaguar... and this morning, as I am sure that you are aware, we announced that the deal on Land Rover would go through' (ibid.) – this last being a reference to Ford's role in acquiring parts of the Rover Group business which BMW was in the process of slicing up, another concern.[10] The Committee too, in the context of a live forum, was dazzled with 'science' – Ford needed 'swing plants'. In these circumstances, not much could be expected by way of immediate retort.

What can readily be admired is the quality of much of the information elicited by the parliamentarians from Ford's representatives appearing before the Committee. Major factory closures by their nature breed disinformation, whether because opinions are freely offered by people not in a position to know, or for other reasons of politic. One explanation of the decision which circulated widely in the aftermath of the announcement was that Ford was unhappy about Britain's decision to stay out of the Euro zone – in the few years prior to the 2000 announcement the pound had appreciated sharply: Ford's president in Europe was cited, at the time and later, as blaming the Dagenham closure on the overly high value of the pound – 'an incredible penalty' (Tolliday 2003: 108). The Committee, backed by Parliament, pressed this point hard; and received a quite unequivocal and wholly contrary reply from Ford's witnesses. Asked 'to what extent has the relationship between the pound and the euro influenced your decisions':

> It has not. The pound is strong today, much stronger than it has been historically, but we did not calculate on the basis of the current value of sterling … [but] a value for sterling that the economists based upon purchasing power parity … a *long-term* view. (HC 2000– 2001: 4) (Citing the response of Mr Ian McAllister, a chairman and managing director of Ford Motor Company Ltd; emphasis added.)

Judgement is still needed here, but the reply is an entirely credible one.[11]

The Committee in live interview, moreover, pressed hard on whether Ford had elected to dispense with its British site because UK-based workers are easier to sack:

> You will have heard the allegations from unions and others that it is easier to sack British workers, cheaper to get rid of UK workers? (Linda Perham MP) (HC 2000–2001: 3)
>
> Could you confirm for me that the statutory requirements in Germany and Britain are considerably dissimilar? (Helen Southworth MP) (ibid.)

And notwithstanding Ford's reply to the effect that it had matched the kind of redundancy payments available in Germany – and had 'consulted' and even put together a 'voluntary social plan' of European standards (HC 2000–2001: 3–4) – the Committee's report, when it came, did at least highlight trade union objections, even noting similar complaints from not dissimilarly positioned workers in other sectors, and concluding that it was indeed factually the case that it is 'easier' and 'cheaper' to dispose of UK employees – for reasons including shorter redundancy requirements, a lack of restrictions and obligations enforceable at law, and lower exit costs (see ibid.: xxxi–xxxii) – albeit with the proviso that these instances did not apply in this particular case (the assurances in this matter from Ford as with the other corporate witnesses being accepted). And the Committee's interrogation did effectively draw out the *volte face* evident in the Ford decision to announce a withdrawal of car assembly from Britain – and impressed by the defence offered that there was a problem of increased fixed costs because of a reduced demand forecast, the company's representatives were gamely criticized for their forecasting errors and grilled on 'gross miscalculation' (ibid.: 2).[12]

But when we come to the Committee's actual adjudication, in the final report written for benefit of Parliament, on the circumstances of the Ford factory closure, some significant signs of an impasse in the scrutiny of corporate activities become evident. The Committee, consistent on this point with Ford's 'swing-plant' defence, argued that it had been revealed that manufacturing 'flexibility' was now the key issue: 'the capacity of one plant to make a range of different models, to switch rapidly from one to another in response to market changes' (HC 2000–2001: xxx) – the Ford swing-plant defence.[13] On this point, we have shown already that the logic of this defence leaves much to explain, because if 'swing-plant economies' exist today, they have always existed, and sacrificed in every instance where a firm organizes production across more than one site. In itself, this is not yet a major criticism of the Committee's report, since an essentially technocratic defence indubitably true insofar as it goes, might cause difficulties for even the most critical judge unrehearsed in the relevant points of analytical interest. But at this point our own judgement of the Ford evidence departs from the Committee's.

What is more problematic is that the Committee's report on this issue then went on to add what can only be described as a positive *embellishment* upon the evidence received, because it made the further claim that British-based sites were therefore simply too inflexible to accommodate more than one product line – and without evidence: 'Ford's immediate choice of sites', the Committee's report observed, 'was probably between Cologne and Dagenham'; and then it went on to offer this conclusion:

> Dagenham was seen by Ford as a relatively old and inflexible plant, although there has been much substantial investment there. It is physically constrained in an awkward site. (ibid.: xii)

And later, and as a more general theme, the point was *embellished* again:

> The implications are grave for older plants, those with geographical constraints or limitations, and those whose internal configuration cannot readily be adapted to the need for flexible plants able to produce several models and switch quickly from one model to another. No matter how flexible and skilled a workforce, the *inherited characteristics* of a plant prove fatal. (ibid.: xxx)

We can compare the first conclusion with what Ford actually said, already alluded to in the sketch of the closure decision in the first section of this chapter:

> It was *not* a question of Dagenham. (HC 2000–2001: 6) (Citing the testimony of Mr Ian McAllister, a Chairman and Managing Director of Ford Motor Company Ltd; emphasis added)

And pressed on whether Ford's past investment strategy for the site, or the geography of the site, or anything about the site itself was an issue, the answer came back:

> There was *no* single reason you can put your finger on and say that is the reason *why* we made the decision we did. (ibid.) (Citing the response of Mr Ian McAllister; emphasis added)

The exchange here concerns the specific choice of Dagenham as the closed site. At this point, we have indicated that a deeper interrogation on 'swing plants' was possible than that to which Ford was subjected: but the issues are relatively technical ones, and even where a reasoned analysis practically compels one to consider employment issues as one of the offsetting factors that *must* be considered by any firm maintaining more than one site – and Ford remained and remains a multiple production sites firm – leeway can certainly be awarded the Committee's report in this regard. But to contradict the apparent terms of evidence received, and in the form moreover of a general formula which could help legitimatize *any* plant closure decision, savours of something else.

And other instances run through the Committee's report: for example, prominence was given in its conclusions to a statement made by one of the Ford witnesses in July 2000 to the Greater London Authority that the Dagenham site was 'the least effective plant that we have in our European operations' (HC 2000–2001: xxx). But in examination before the committee a quite different inference had already been conceded.[14] The parliamentarian sitting on the committee representing as her constituents many of the workers affected by the Ford closure decision had obtained productivity comparisons between Dagenham and Cologne which placed the UK site ahead of the German site in the company's own estimates shortly before the closure announcement; and on this point the Ford witnesses did not appear to directly demur on the information put to them: 'Dagenham did improve its productivity and efficiency, but so did Cologne ... a dynamic change and both operations *were* improving radically' (HC 2000–2001: 6). (Citing the reply of Mr Ian McAllister to the direct question of Linda Perham MP; emphasis added.) Again, the presentation of the Committee's report could be challenged.

But only when we consider the questions not asked do we get a full sense of some of the ellipses in the tack taken by the parliamentary committee. Ford had given assurances to its Dagenham workforce on the guaranteed future of the car assembly site as recently as one year previous to the closure announcement (HC 2000–2001: 6). We observed, however, when setting out the preliminary facts of the case and key points of evidence, that relations between Ford and its Dagenham workforce were less than tranquil. Indeed, less than two months prior to the closure announcement, it was reported in the media that the then education and employment minister (Margaret Hodge MP) received a warning from Ford executives that its Dagenham workers were 'too aggressive', 'failed to support the company', and represented by unions that 'resisted change'.[15] The general theme was taken up by one of the committee's members (again, Linda Perham), who noted that on a tour of the Dagenham site undertaken on the day before Ford appeared before the committee the view had again been obtained from Ford management that 'cooperation', 'culture change', and 'competitive performance' – the latter statement contradicted, we could perhaps note, by the data put to the Ford witnesses by the same MP the next day – had 'regrettably' not been achieved (HC 2000–2001: 6). Asked to respond, the answer came back that it was a 'minor issue', and that the key thing was consolidation to obtain the advantages of swing-plant facilities (ibid.: 6–7). There the matter dropped.

But the details of industrial relations at the Dagenham site at this time surely demanded a further inquiry (a point, we should note, which is not a criticism of this last MP). In 1999, in the year before the factory closure, an industrial relations tribunal upheld a case taken by a Ford worker concerning racial harassment within the Ford Dagenham engine plant. This fuelled a strike by workers led from the adjacent car assembly plant to protest against tolerance of racism, and to widely reported meetings between the then head of the Transport and General Workers Union (TGWU) Bill Morris, the first black leader of a major British trade union, and Ford. A few years earlier, seven Asian and African-Caribbean workers had received substantial compensation, again on grounds of racial discrimination, this time concerning hiring practices at the Dagenham complex – while almost *half* of the Dagenham complex were recruited from ethnic minorities, concentrated most particularly in the car assembly plant, these workers could not access better paid jobs at the site as a whole. Bill Morris was widely quoted at the time as complaining about compliance within the site to unacceptable practices. One year earlier, the company had again been obliged to pay compensation, after superimposing white faces on African-Caribbean and Asian workers in advertising copy.[16]

But here nothing was asked by the committee in oral cross-examination. And in the Committee's report, the one comment on the race issue at Dagenham was ambiguous:

> Its past history of industrial relations has been troubled, with allegations of absenteeism. It has gained unfavourable publicity with allegations of racism. (HC 2000–2001: xii)

If we step back to conclude now, two different kinds of observation and reflection are called for, each of which picks up a theme from the previous chapter. The first is simply the workaday question of how transnational producers organize their assets from the vantage point of the privileged position which they occupy regarding the leverage they may exert over parties with which they deal. These parties include governments in host economies, some of the more domestically rooted small firms and businesses with which they may deal, and, not least, trade unions and workers. The analysis undertaken with regards to intersecting aggregate scale curves in the previous section in order to make sense of and contextualize Ford's evidence, and viewed as a more general prospectus, is consistent with a transnational's bargaining advantages. Certainly corporations incur avoidable costs whenever they subdivide production, but the fact that they routinely do so points to other advantages which they then obtain. The interest in our construction lies less in any attempt to employ it to provide a definite answer as to what finally motivated Ford's decision – demand factors, comparative ease and cheapness of sacking, and industrial relations could *all* play important roles in the scenario which Ford's own evidence invites us to consider – but rather to show that the context within which these various considerations are played out is wholly consistent with a worldview in which transnational producers *do* organize to pressure labour. The question is not therefore simply why Dagenham *rather* than Cologne, but rather why begin in the first instance *with* a Dagenham, a Cologne, and a Valencia – especially in the context of a fully integrated and European theatre of operation, as Ford now enjoys. Whether Ford really did change its long-term demand forecasts, or whether the key factor was the deteriorating situation in its UK industrial relations, are moot. The technocratic invocation of 'swing plants' and 'flexibility' is a side issue, not a main feature; the reference above to Glyn's observances on a world of threats is more telling.

But of even greater import for our purposes is what a parliamentary committee made of the case, in a context informed by Mrs Thatcher's inheritance, of Tony Blair's early promise that Britain would continue to excel internationally in the lack of protection afforded its workers, and by a grown national dependence on the course of private investment decisions by potentially footloose transnational corporations. And here the answer might reasonably be said to be just about what could be expected. In a world not only of threats but also of future promises – Ford took care to withdraw only Ford-badged cars from

Dagenham: the site still exists to produce Ford engines – there may be palpable limits to how far even the most dogged parliamentarians are liable to go.

Lean production: Britain's manufacturing renaissance

We began this chapter by stating that there was much of particular interest to learn about the character of capitalism as it exists in Britain today by considering how the state chooses to respond to public policy setbacks, the context in this instance being one in which all of its main political parties have acceded to a common view on the factors most liable to attract investment from potentially footloose firms; but to this stage we have focused on the evidence obtained by an investigating parliamentary committee from two of the principals, Ford Motors and the Ford unions, and the ellipses evident in its responses to this evidence – but what of the relevant government department?

At the point when the loss of car assembly operations at Ford Dagenham was announced, policy thinking at the (since renamed) Department of Trade and Industry (DTI)[17] was heavily weighted by two assumptions vis-à-vis manufacturing. The first was that in addition to the immediate gains to production and employment that could be achieved via the medium of inward foreign direct investment, the porosity of the British economy with respect to the sourcing activities of transnational firms with an international sphere of operations meant that 'best practices' would disseminate to the United Kingdom, and with the automotive industry deemed to be a leading sector. Both points featured heavily in the department's submission to the committee, which stressed the leading status of Britain as a recipient of inward foreign direct investment – home to seven foreign owned and 'major' vehicle manufacturers, and with over 2000 enterprises linked in via component parts and accessories (HC 2000–2001: 94–5) – and the supposedly transformative powers of the spread of 'best practices' via this medium. In this last respect, the role of entrants from Japan was highlighted, and with particular regard to the benefits thereby achieved via the (alleged) introduction and spread of (so-called) 'lean production':

> The advent of Japanese vehicle manufacturing transplants in the UK, starting with the arrival of Nissan in 1986, has...provided the opportunity for a whole generation of UK managers to

understand the principles and practices of lean manufacture. (HC 2000–2001: 95)

By implication, the downside risk of a porous economy, namely that the same footloose corporations can easily take jobs elsewhere instead, was more than balanced by the successes achieved by attracting new inward investors like the Japanese car makers. Indeed, the thrust of the DTI response was that the sector as a whole, with car production recently the highest it had been 'since 1972' (sic), and with record exports, had proved to be 'one of the major UK success stories of recent years' (ibid.: 94). It was also noted that the United Kingdom was the largest venue for inward investment in Europe in this sector.

Now we have previously noted (in Chapter 2) a growing emphasis within UK industrial policy with reference to manufacturing, throughout the Thatcher era, on advertising the attractiveness of the economy to international investors; and not least from Japan, as reflected in the mania for all production practices (allegedly) Japanese. But whether this boast should have been delivered in such sanguine terms to a parliamentary committee – in circumstances, moreover, that were so embarrassing – is doubtful. If we take the year of the Ford closure announcement (2000) as a reference point, and consider a four-year window on either side, the data are consistent with two things: however looked at, the total industry contribution to the UK economy was flat, or even declining – stagnant might be an appropriate word – while the balance of trade steadily worsened. After a brief rise prior to the reference year, industry gross value added (GVA) for UK auto products as a whole (including parts) fell, as indeed it did for the major subcomponents of the sector like vehicles and engines. While employment fell steadily, consistent with some broad increase in labour productivity, there is no evidence that such changes as were realized translated into an enhanced industry income. Total industry production in both cars and commercial vehicles (CVs), while a subset of the sector, was similarly stagnant. And in every product category, tyres, auto-electrical, vehicles, bodies, and parts, the net trade position, showing a worsening trade deficit overall, deteriorated. Moreover, if we look again at the boast made by the DTI that car (not commercial vehicle) production was at its highest level since almost 30 years previously, one cannot but consider the implied contraction of the sector, in absolute numbers

Table 3.1 Performance indicators for UK (all) automotive manufacture

	1996	1998	2000	2002	2004
Gross Value Added (GVA) (1996 base)	1.00	1.12	0.84	0.95	0.95
Employment (000s):	288	293	263	243	221
Production (000s):					
Cars	1,686	1,761	1,641	1,630	1,647
Commercial Vehicles (CVs)	238	215	172	191	209

Source: Based on Department of Business Enterprise and Regulatory Reform (ONS data).

Table 3.2 Balance of trade in UK (all) automotive manufacture

	1996	1998	2000	2002	2004
Overall balance of trade (£M):	–5,941	–7,319	–7,167	–12,161	–12,884

Source: Based on Department of Business Enterprise and Regulatory Reform (ONS data).

of cars made, in the interim – even before considering the issue in terms of *global* output shares. Similarly, while 'record exports' sound promising, the world similarly expands and grows, and these were still far from adequate when set against imports.

Some sample statistics for the indicators just noted – commencing ten years or so after Nissan's arrival in Britain, and showing, one supposes, the effects of the lean manufacturing revolution – are set out in Tables 3.1 and 3.2.[18] At a glance, it can be seen that our comments on these indicators are borne out in the data. But if things might have looked better, even at the point of the DTI submission (made in July 2000) this was already known, because almost immediately after the boasts that the auto industry was not just one of the great UK success stories but also a world leader in lean production – a 'leading practitioner of lean manufacturing' as the DTI put it (HC 2000–2001: 95) – the same DTI memorandum went almost immediately on to add a proviso:

Despite the improvements in productivity made in recent years by vehicle manufacturers and by many component suppliers, the

UK's overall productivity (measured by Gross Value Added per person) is *lower* than that of our main competitors in the EU. *This is a situation similar to that in some other sectors of manufacturing.* (HC 2000–2001: 96; emphasis added)

This qualification, a sad one indeed, is noted in Coffey (2006) – 'Britain is thus doubly distinguished when set against its main European partners and rivals, contriving somehow to have both the leanest producers and also the least productive' (ibid.: 133).

If one asks what the evidence at this time was of 'lean' benefits, the answer is none; but nonetheless, the DTI response to the Trade and Industry Committee is highly instructive, because it highlights as much as the Committee's report the impasse reached by the politics of competitiveness as it applies to the United Kingdom. As we observed in the previous chapter, the UK-based automotive sector is exceedingly internationalized; and the flipside to the boast that Britain is Europe's major venue for inward investment may be a situation in which little else *could* be said by the DTI without seeming to attack the trajectory of industrial policy towards manufacture of the past several or more decades. In this connection, the conjuration of a 'lean revolution' makes sense only in context of this awkward position: if not quite a fig leaf, then at least unevidenced optimism.[19]

It is perhaps unfortunate that as well as avoiding any direct questions on race relations at the Ford Dagenham site the parliamentary committee did not ask either the management or unions about their take on lean production. As it happens, part of the workplace tensions at Dagenham revolved around the implementation of a signed agreement between Ford and the unions – a 'Memorandum of Understanding' – which tied the company into honouring existing agreements undertaken with plant unions not to undermine terms or conditions of work. The unions would for their part facilitate changes that would not, by their implementation, breach this agreement. The document in question, put together by experienced union negotiators, invoked lean production: 'the unions must be alive to the issues that lean production creates…this Memorandum of Understanding outlines and confirms the minimum standards/ protections that are agreed between the Company and the Unions' (Ford Blue Book 1997: 146). This document, which committed Ford not to degrade working terms and conditions, or to undermine or attempt to bypass union organization, quickly became a point of active contention.[20] But whether realities on the ground would be of any real interest to the DTI concerning the phenomenon of 'lean production' may be to rather miss the point.

Summing up

In this chapter we encounter a site closure decision by a major transnational corporation operating in Europe as a US foreign direct investor and employing a number of plant sites spread across countries. The decision of Ford Motors to withdraw fully from the assembly of Ford-badged cars in Britain provides a pressure point from which to consider motives and responses, our principal concern being with what we can learn from this case about the character of British capitalism today. The permissive stance of successive UK governments, both Conservative and Labour, to the exit as well as the entry decisions of transnational firms is not in dispute. But we can observe the response at a moment of public policy scrutiny and pressure to consider not only how the still young New Labour government responded in a moment of crisis – as expressed, for example, in the response of the then Department of Trade and Industry – but also to ask whether, given the policy inheritance from previous governments, even parliament's watchdogs on government policy retain a capacity for critical assessment when confronted with circumstances of the kind surrounding this setback. Viewed solely as a plant closure exercise, the Ford case is an amply revealing one, because the details take us straight to the criticism that large firms maintain a network of cross-border sites for reasons best understood as the bargaining leverages thereby obtained. But more fundamentally, and in a case framed by issues of class and race, the quality of the evidence obtained in this instance by an investigating parliamentary committee far exceeded any subsequent willingness to explore what was uncovered; and the government departmental response in this instance suggests less a reasoned argument than a defensive reflex conditioned by UK dependence on inward investment. The details of the case reflect badly on the realities of the working experiences and prospects of the memberships of Britain's industrial trade unions, in a context defined by a thoroughgoing 'national' reliance on the merits of a 'porous' economy.

Addendum: a technical note on scale curves and throughput variety

The scale curves employed in this chapter make several kinds of abstraction. As described in a previous chapter vis-à-vis the content of the post-Fordism debate, car assembly lines, as with many assembly-line systems, typically process a range of model specifications: cars which differ in body, engine, equipment and trim, interior and exterior colours, and so forth. Since to consider this feature would greatly complicate the analysis but without altering any of the essential points made in this present chapter, we have abstracted from the particular technical issues raised by throughput variety. In effect, we assume that each car built, regardless of specification, incurs the same direct and indirect wage cost to produce, at least insofar as the assembly plant is concerned. Cost differences arising would therefore follow only from differences in component parts bought out – a separate category of cost and one not germane to the problem at hand. The level of the wage cost in each case is of course a function of variables that we do consider in this chapter, focusing on plant structures and tacit wage-effort bargaining. While abstracting from throughput variety in the course of our analysis is a technical simplification, we should note that the Ford executives' evidence discussed in this chapter makes the same abstraction, as indeed do most industry forecasts. In fact, a second type of abstraction with respect to throughput variety is often made in such instances, namely that differences across car lines are also abstracted from – this is true whenever discussion is set at the general level of global demand, capacity, etc. In our scale curve analysis, and for tractability of diagrammatic representation as well as of consistency with the verbal submissions made by the Ford executives, we make this second kind of abstraction as well: here, we assume that each car built within the envisaged complex of car assembly plants – once the number of sites is determined – is projected to require a similar wage cost to produce, regardless of identity. Because each car built will add (by assumption) the same amount to the company wage bill, it is then permissible to draw a global scale curve with total output counted in 'cars'.

For readers interested in the algebra of the stylized scale curve analysis set out in the first of the two cost curve diagrams in the main text (Figure 3.1), the intersection point between curves XX and curve YY is determined as follows:

$$Q^* = (f_m - f_n) / (w_n - w_m) > 0$$

where Q^* is the critical number of forecast units at which cost projections are the same regardless of the planned number of sites (as per Figure 3.1); f is the relevant aggregate fixed cost and w the relevant wage cost each indexed against the number of sites to be operated, shown in this instance as a choice between m or n sites. If we suppose that m is larger than n (or $m > n$) then the numerator on the right hand side of the expression above will be positive because running with more sites rather than fewer increases the sum of fixed (and overhead) costs ($f_m > f_n$); but at the same time, the denominator is also positive, provided that spreading the work across a larger number of sites is expected to reduce unit wage cost ($w_n > w_m$), so that Q^* is positive: the actual point at which Q^* is identified depends on the state of expectation at play at the time of decision making.

The use of scale curves in economics is, of course, commonplace and generic: but the interested reader wishing to consider this kind of construct in more detail can consult Coffey and Tomlinson (2006), which also makes use of aggregate scale curves but constructed on a more general *a priori* basis regarding fixed costs and wage costs and therfore allowing of different kinds of interpretation and application.

4
The Self-Effacing State: Private Services Required

Nobody writing a year ago predicted the events which would see the Bush administration in the United States resort to substantial nationalization as a means of saving the US economy from financial collapse. Nor did anyone foresee the government of Gordon Brown in Britain threaten banks and other institutions with nationalization should they fail to take steps to support the British housing market and to supply credit to struggling firms – in a context where a run on one bank had already seen it brought into public ownership; nor would it have been easy to imagine Wall Street and the City responding without outrage. Were one to step back in time just a little further, confidence, in any of these quarters, in the unshakeable foundations of the market would, no doubt, have been palpable. And even now it is too soon to say whether the manifest conviction displayed until recently by prominent figures associated with the New Labour project in all aspects of the market will be severely tarnished when it comes to state services provision. At the time of writing, there is talk of further UK privatization with the planned involvement of a private (Dutch) firm in the management of business in that long-serving but long-suffering British national institution, the Post Office.

The line of demarcation separating activities organized by the state from activities organized in the private sector became a highly charged public policy issue because of successive waves of privatization undertaken from the 1980s, the impact of which upon organized labour we have already touched upon. The retrospective endorsement given Mrs Thatcher's efforts by Tony Blair, and the continuation of pro-privatization and pro-market liberalization policies under each of his governments, has been considered by many a defining feature of New Labour – more so even than adherence to deregulated labour markets and an open-door policy to international investment for internationally traded goods and services, for the simple reason that most public services provision is delivered *in situ*. Cross-border firms may be part of a growing body of interests lobbying for state contracts, but the services in question are not per se suitable for trade across national borders. This distinction gives a particular cast to issues of public services privatization.

In this chapter we appraise the so-called Private Finance Initiative (PFI), an experiment in further extending the reach of private profit-seeking firms into public sector services provision, existing in muted form before the election of Tony Blair's first government, but greatly extended in size and scope since. This, it might initially be thought, is a dry and unpromising venue at which to pause; or, rather, that it is a policy about which little more can be said other than that critics despise it. But upon consideration there are peculiar features to the PFI that are quite remarkable. Because in addition to the bearing which this policy has upon the real state of the UK public finances – suddenly topical – it could hardly have been more thoughtfully constructed had the planned intent been to answer a question of deep and profound interest to social and political scientists as well as public administrators and economists. If the conviction motivating the PFI is really that private sector management is more efficient than public, just how large would this assumed performance gap have to be before the PFI makes 'sense' – in other words, just how far has the British state gone in claiming its *own* incompetence: in transport, in education, in healthcare, indeed, in a myriad of other social functions.

A break from the trend

In framing this question we should first take stock of the fact that if policy today is formulated in a context informed by strong convictions about the manifold inadequacies of public versus private sector organization, these convictions are themselves certainties of very recent origin. For example, even a brief excursion into the literature of the 1960s or 1970s on trends evident within mature capitalist economies provides many instances of writers convinced of the inevitability of a growing state involvement in economic provision, so much so that the 'ideology' of late capitalism could be deemed by some to include intellectual accommodations to the 'hypertrophy' of the state, and not least in Western Europe.[1] Such views were informed by a complex of factors: by existing state responsibilities for providing or maintaining a variety of institutions and services; by past state acquisitions of, or support for, privately operated industries in strategically 'failing' or 'undeveloped' sectors; and also, at least for critics on the left, a sense of decrepitude in the system as a whole that could only invoke further state involvement in private commercial activities – fed in the United Kingdom by a struggling 'domestic' manufacturing sector and the lobbying of some afflicted interests for nationalization. Similar thoughts can no doubt be found amongst more conservative writers of the period, albeit with a different balance of hopes and fears as to the likely progress of events.

From a different perspective, an historical précis of the history of twentieth-century public ownership in Britain has led a more recent writer, in a comprehensive survey of the economic impact of UK privatizations from the 1980s onwards, to assess previous developments – before the historical impress of Mrs Thatcher – in terms consistent with a long swing towards deepening state involvement in the organization of the economy. In this major survey, now compulsory for students of this topic, and which warns against schismatic readings, Florio (2004) proposes that an observer, commencing with the later nineteenth century, would see a discernible Victorian welfare state, and a growing municipal sector, segue into a more developed government presence and a gradual shifting of boundaries towards greater state activity. Growing provisions prior to the First World War, in areas like education, health, pensions and labour protection, were followed by a considerable extension of state intervention during the war itself. After the subsequent ebb there came further flows, into the management of education, health, welfare, and industrial relations, as well as intervention in key industries – coal, steel, rail, shipbuilding, cotton (ibid.: 2–13). Prior at least to the outbreak of the Great War, the processes by which state involvement in the economy grew are argued as best described in terms less of a definitive shift in the boundaries between public and private, but more rather of processes of 'symbiosis' and 'coevolution' – 'an independent evolution of the British institutions and of the mentality of those who had to run them, in a context in which one clearly saw the tangible shortfall of private action in many fields' (ibid.: 11–2).

Even when a further advance in the experience of state involvement in the economy during the Second World War was followed, in
1945, by the 'pro-public ownership' Labour government of Clement
Attlee, Florio is loathe to conceive of the trend towards growing state
involvement in the economy in schismatic terms: even these years
are described as being as much an 'epilogue of a long season that
started in the early Victorian era', as the 'beginning of a new phase'
(Florio 2004: 16–17). This is an interesting judgement. Over and
above the major impetus given public sector provision in areas like
health, education, and welfare – Britain's National Health Service
(NHS) was, it will be remembered, founded in 1948 – these years
also saw many of the major utilities brought within national public
frameworks, as well as the nationalization of industries (some with a
complex history of intervention) previously operated by private sector firms producing and selling goods and services.

In Florio's view, there was only a partial overlap between advancing 'socialist sentiments' and a growing state involvement in provision of services and goods. The private sector conceded to public
forms of organization over a sufficiently long period for causes other
than an extended suffrage or emerging party colours to be evident.
The 'partisan dimension was not as important as one might think',
there being a 'broad consensus', following war-time economic administration, on 'state led reconstruction and rationalisation' (Florio
2004: 16–19). While coal, civil aviation, transport, electricity, gas,
and steel were successively established as major public industries by
post-war Labour governments, and further programmes of nationalization later undertaken by Labour in shipbuilding and aerospace,
little effort was made by Conservative governments from the 1950s
through the 1970s to undo the 'public economy': the Wilson government of 1968 renationalized the steel industry which had been
previously 'denationalized', in 1952, by Winston Churchill, but it
was Edward Heath's Conservative government which nationalized
water (in 1973), and which sought to secure Jaguar cars by bringing
the firm into public ownership.

There is no doubt an interesting debate to be had as to the extent
to which this perspective is compatible with the 'hypertrophy' thesis. The febrile atmosphere evident in the 1970s – an increasingly
vocal left-wing movement calling for radical extensions of state
ownership as a vehicle for industrial democracy, overlapped with

business interests seeking state bailouts or even nationalization as a way of pushing the costs of corporate run-downs onto taxpayers, and with some sections of the labour movement correspondingly wary of state takeovers[2] – plays a part in the formulations of the first kind of assessment, with which Florio, focusing on actual movements in the boundaries of state ownership, is less concerned. Certainly the politics of the period are important from the viewpoint of later political trajectories: a reaction within sections of the Conservative party to the Heath nationalizations undoubtedly played a part in the internal history of Thatcherism. But from either viewpoint, the subsequent fact of the 'Great Divestiture', Florio's apt term for the privatizations of the Thatcher governments of the 1980s and beyond, are all the more dramatic.

Looking back, it is still possible to be surprised at the scale of the endeavour. If we take advantage of the tables and summary by Florio (2004: 24–44), then the key features of this progression, vis-à-vis sales of state assets, are as follows. During the term of the first Thatcher government (1979–1983), only a dozen or so, and in these cases relatively smaller businesses, were 'partially or totally privatised'; during the second term of office (1983–1987) privatization commenced for some quite major companies, and for about twice as many businesses, including the regional electrical companies as well as water and sewage; after a third successive election victory, leading to five more years (1987–1992) of Conservative government, the process continued, and with another increase in the number of privatized businesses. Further privatizations initiated by John Major in the fourth and final Conservative period in office included a substantially shrunken coal industry and rail. The number of enterprises sold and their range of activity was formidable, reflecting the past accretion to the state of economic organization in a variety of sectors, but with a predominance in a handful of strategic sectors – 'energy, transport equipment and services, telecommunications, and water' (Florio 2004: 30) – and with giant privatizations including British Gas, British Telecom, and the electric grid, boosting sales receipts. Florio estimates 'gross receipts from the divestiture of public corporations and sale of debt' (ibid.) over this period (at 1995 prices) at £86B.

For a subsequent wave of critical commentary from the left – that part, so to speak, not committed to the concept of a post-Fordist era of reflexive accumulation – this divestiture has frequently been described in terms evoking plunder. Thus, for example, the far from weakly evidenced judgement of Andrew Glyn:

> The big gainers from privatization were those that 'stagged' the issues of shares (selling them for a quick profit), the firms in the City which earned large fees from arranging the privatizations and management, whose pay was ratcheted up'. (Glyn 2006: 40)

For Florio, approaching the matter from a different tack, and informed both by the rhetoric of the privatization programmes and a long historical purview, and warning specifically against any search for a simple motive like improved economic efficiency, the 'neoliberal agenda' has the sense of a revivalism:

> [P]rivatisation was in fact part of a broader agenda. If we look back to the parallel growth pattern of industry and state in Britain since early Victorian times, the neoliberal agenda was probably more than a break in the postwar social policy. It was an ambitious attempt to revive a golden age of individualism, reversing a secular trend. Privatization should be examined as part of this public policy project. (Florio 2004: 29)

All of which is consistent with the kind of 'shock' thesis explored in an earlier chapter – a massive divestiture of state assets, gathering pace over time.[3]

Such indeed, is the apparent break with the long swing towards public ownership evident over a much longer period in both the United Kingdom and elsewhere, that there are serious dangers of oversimplifying the changing boundaries of the state. The regulation of privatized utilities was quickly forced on government in Britain – as in other countries – as the likely consequences of laissez faire became more apparent.[4] And in any case, most of the privatized enterprises in Britain 'fell' into state hands only as a past consequence of private sector failures or collapse – the not so-hidden history of capitalism, coming once again to the fore with the current financial crisis. Moreover, the public sector in the United Kingdom, even after the 'withdrawal' of sections of industry and the major utilities, remains massively important in services provision; and notwithstanding the impacts of the public sector outsourcing programmes which added so much to the travails of labour from the Thatcher years onwards, as a source of employment – not least for women – the public sector remains very large.

But the divestiture was nonetheless a real and substantial one, and Britain undoubtedly exercises a wider international influence too both from the viewpoint of the methods it employed when privatizations took place (see Florio 2004: 30) but also in terms of the principle itself – the political demonstration effect. As Glyn observes, and in a book which we should remember surveys *all* of the globe's advanced capitalisms, the UK case was a 'trailblazer' in this kind of state divestiture, an international 'paragon' for this kind of example of the removal of 'state control' (Glyn 2006: 37).

We observed in a previous chapter that Tony Blair's first government was anxious to impress upon the business community that it would 'minimise the impact on business' of any labour market reforms – '[if] there was to be partnership, it was partnership within the existing structures of authority and reward, in the manner of its Conservative predecessors' (Coates 2005c: 85). Perhaps the first point of note on the general question of privatization and appropriate roles for the public sphere is the fact that equally quick assurances were given on the question of nationalization: thus the first Blair government snubbed calls to reverse the privatization of rail, the processes of which overlapped inconveniently with the demise of the Major government. The second is that little doubt was left as to the strength of conviction that was going to be expressed about the comparative efficiency of private sector management,

> Where there is no over-riding reason for preferring the public provision of goods and services ... then the presumption should be that economic activity is *best* left to the private sector with market forces being *fully* encouraged to operate. (Tony Blair cited in *Guardian* 8th April 1997; also cited in Coates 2005c: 48; emphasis added)

It is in each of these contexts that we turn now to the study of the PFI policy initiative, a scheme which both in its conception and in its implementation offers a rare instance in which it is possible to probe deeply into what a firm conviction favouring private sector efficacies can mean in policy practice; and a scheme moreover which is again being taken up in other countries following the UK demonstration. In this last regard, and in a wider global setting characterized by continuing pressures for market liberalization by national governments from organizations and agreements like the World Trade Organization (WTO) and the General Agreement on Trade in Services (GATS)[5], we might note reported PFI-style undertakings (as well as other forms of 'Public–Private Partnership' contracts) in countries including Australia, Canada, Finland, France, Ireland, Japan, Netherlands, Norway, and Portugal.

Private services required

There are really two main aspects to the Private Finance Initiative (or PFI), as an exercise in public sector financing and management. First, a private sector contractor or consortium undertakes to finance and organize a capital investment project, the services of which – the use of the asset – are then leased to the public sector. In other words, the public sector purchases a flow of services from a capital investment project organized by private firms and funded using privately generated finance. Second, services provision in the post-construction operational phase of the project is then also typically subcontracted to, or via, the same private sector firms. In this way, the following aspects of public services provision are changed by the PFI: it changes the basis upon which investment in capital projects, deemed necessary by the state for reasons of public services provision, is financed; it changes too the initial organization of these projects, and the extent to which provision of related services in their operational phase is then subcontracted to the private sector. The public sector thereby engages the private sector not only to 'finance', but also to 'design, construct or refurbish' facilities as well as providing related 'support services', under what is typically a long-term contract (Pollock and Price 2004; see also Sawyer 2003). In most cases, public funding takes the form of annual payments – or 'unitary charge' – commencing in the project's operational phase (Pollock and Price 2004: 10).

One immediate issue of note is the size of the scheme, because it is evident from even a brief survey of the literature, often very critical, that the longer-term impact of the initiative in terms of its magnitude and scope is potentially underestimated. Since its inception, the scheme has grown quickly and substantially, and this is generally understood. But as Sawyer (2003: 173–5) observes, how 'big' the initiative looks will vary as to whether one considers it relative to other forms of public sector investment considered as *gross* investment or *net* investment. Because gross investment figures are calculated inclusive of spending needed simply to maintain an existing public sector capital stock, a comparison of PFI with net public sector investment will give a better proximate indicator of the transformation of the public sphere and the importance of 'private' projects within. And so while most commentators reckon investment by PFI as being in the region of 10 to 15 per cent of investment contracted by the public sector, Sawyer's estimate is substantially higher reckoned in *net* terms *at around one quarter* – 25 per cent – of the 'overall net investment contracted by the public sector' (ibid.): a very sizeable contribution. If maintained over a long enough time span, the eventual transformative effect of PFI on the composition of the organization of ownerships and responsibilities would be far more substantial that is generally supposed, even by critics of the scheme.[6] Broken down by government department, the PFI scheme has been most heavily relied upon for spending by local authorities (for projects including schools), followed by transport, local government and the regions, with health in third place (ibid.).

One major criticism of this approach to public services funding is that the future commitments of the state with regard to the private sector from the PFI are not counted as part of the current public sector borrowing requirement: so far as the national debt is concerned, these future payments have been placed 'off balance sheet'. Controversy over the abuse of political expediency, and mounting long-term risk, of this kind of off-sheet borrowing by government has increased. Sawyer (2003: 176) estimates that had future liabilities incurred via the PFI been obtained via bond issues on the terms then available to government – at the time of his own calculation – then the addition to the official national debt would have easily exceeded a publicly reported fall; it would have added 'significantly', in the order of 20 to 25 per cent, and (on trend) rising. At the present time of writing, official debt is expected to escalate very significantly, a consequence of the sharp downturn in the economy, the borrowing required to bail out sections of the private banking and finance sector – and possibly other sections of the economy – and a hurried 'rediscovery' of 'Keynesian' macroeconomics. But these last are points to which we return in a later chapter; we focus now on another issue.

At one level, the organization of PFI ventures can, in practical terms, be exceedingly complex affairs: contracts are awarded in the first instance to a consortium of firms that may in turn elect to sub-contract much or all of the work required by the project vis-à-vis design and construction, while obtaining the finance required to fund this work from a variety of sources. Similarly, subcontracting arrangements may also pertain in the operational phase of the project. The increased transactional complexity (as a cost issue) and potential loss of transparency (as a governance issue) have been two major areas of criticism. In this respect, a full understanding of the network of private sector inputs and liabilities may require in some instances the patience and competence of a forensically minded accountant.[7] But at the same time, the issue that we now wish to explore can be understood at quite a general level of abstraction, and can be posed as a simple question, thus: How *inefficient* would public sector organization of investment projects have to be, given the rates of return expected on capital invested by the participating PFI consortiums, before this route to public services provision makes sense in terms of its comparative cost?

A thought experiment

Suppose we begin with a thought experiment. Imagine a hypothetical scenario in which a state body commits to making a stream of future payments to the successful winner of a tender to organize, on behalf of the state, a capital project, and in exchange for the future services that will then be provided to the state via this project. In our hypothesized world the amounts of these projected expenditures are announced by the state in advance of the award of a contract to the successful bidder, and are to be treated as a firm commitment: future payments will be the same irrespective of which bidder wins the contract. The decision as to which bidder wins the contract will then reflect expectations of the quantity and quality of services to be provided – or the quantity measured in some appropriate 'quality unit'. For example, if the projected lifespan of the capital project in its operational phase is n years, we might imagine the state body announcing at the outset of the tendering process what the payment is going to be in each year in exchange for the services of the project – and then considering which amongst the competing bidders is likely to offer most in return.

Let us stretch our assumptions a little further by supposing that the rate of return expected by each bidder is known to all parties, as is the organizational capacity of each, and that there are no moral hazard issues (nobody cheats). Finally, let us assume that there are two contending bids, consortium A and consortium B. Each will undertake to organize the project and then lease its services back to the state, but A is only willing to do so in exchange for a 'high' expected rate of return, r_A, while B will do so in exchange for a 'low' return, r_B. Remembering that the state intends to award the contract to the bidder (in this hypothetical world) that promises to offer it most in exchange for its money, the question we pose is this: if in this scenario the bid from consortium A were preferred over B, what would this imply about the assumption the state is making about their respective organizational capabilities? We could infer that the ostensibly 'cheaper' bidder is held to be less organizationally effective. If the award goes to consortium A in preference to consortium B, the state in this example could reasonably be construed as signalling that A is more efficient than B.

Our interest in this thought experiment is by analogy, because the position of the private sector consortium which wins a PFI contract, in preference to a state-funded programme with capital raised via direct bond issues, is analogous to that of the ostensibly more expensive bid in our example which nonetheless wins the contract. This is because from the viewpoint of the state when it awards a PFI contract to an organizing consortium of firms, the implicit cost of the capital raised on its behalf is the real rate of return expected by the organizing consortium of firms. From this private firms in question will defray both their own future profits plus interest payments to investors who have supplied private funds for the project. On the other hand, the cost of capital to the state from bond issues is simply the real post-tax rate of return on government bonds (see Sawyer 2003: 177); and this is known to have been lower than the expected returns of private sector firms involved in PFI schemes throughout the period in which the initiative has grown.[8] One inference might then be – if the PFI scheme is not simply 'off-sheet' borrowing – that in contests for state-awarded contracts the ostensibly 'cheaper' route of in-house provision has lost out to the private sector because the state deems public sector management to be less organizationally effective when compared to what private firms do.

The same point can be put another way. Had the *same* stream of future liabilities outstanding on PFI contracts resulted from government borrowing on terms defined by the real post-tax rate of return on new debt issues, the real value today of the resources being committed by the state to public sector projects would be larger because of a smaller discount factor for the returns expected by investors. If the decision of the body awarding the PFI contract is interpreted as *signalling* a view on the comparative organizational efficiency of private versus public sector management then *a view is taken that the private sector will deliver more than the state would be able to.*

To develop this point further let us return to our hypothesized world. We can infer from the terms of our example that the state views consortium A in preferential terms as regards to its organizational capabilities in organizing a capital project. This is because the real resource which consortium A will undertake to commit to the project today in return for the future and committed stream of payments from the state is known to be less that the real resource which its rival (consortium B) will commit; because in return for the *same* set of future payments A expects a *higher* rate of return.

We can capture this point visually by means of a simple diagram. The real resource that will be committed today by each consortium is found by discounting the future payments from the state (for later use of the capital project) using the rates of return which each consortium expects to earn by putting money into the capital project. In general terms, for any future stream of payments the discounted present value of that stream will fall the higher the discount factor used to calculate its real value today: in terms of Figure 4.1, the relationship will be a simple curve like CC.[9]

Remembering that in our hypothesized world the state first announces the stream of payments and then awards the contract to the consortium from which it expects most, we can then see exactly why consortium A is deemed to be more organizationally efficient. Once the future commitment of the state is known, curve CC is fixed in position. If discounting using the high rate of return expected by A (r_A), we can plot against this curve the corresponding size of the real resource it is prepared to commit: since the actual values in this instance are arbitrary, let us call this V_A. If instead we were to discount

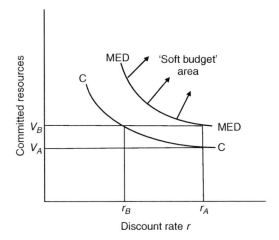

Figure 4.1   Organizational efficiency comparisons

using the low rate of return expected by B (r_B), we could again plot against this curve the corresponding size of the real resource it is prepared to commit; and again, since the actual sums are arbitrary, let us call this V_B. And because firm A expects most profit to be earned on its investment in the capital project, and in exchange for the given future stream of payments committed to by the state, it follows that its willingness to commit real resources today is smallest: as a result, because r_A is greater than r_B, it follows conversely that V_A is less than V_B. And if in these circumstances the state selects consortium A anyway, it follows that the state must believe that there is something less organizationally effective about consortium B.

We can gauge the minimum extent of the assumed difference in comparative organizational efficiencies with reference again to Figure 4.1. If we use for this purpose the difference between V_A and V_B proportionate to V_A – using the intended real resource commitment of the *successful* consortium as the base point of comparison – then we can capture this proportionate difference visually as follows. In the diagram a second curve MED can be added with the property that the vertical distance between it and curve CC at the point where the discount rate is r_A is just equal to the difference between V_A and V_B, while the height here of CC is just equal to V_A: the same proportionate relationships are maintained along the length of the MED curve. The larger the minimum extent of the assumed difference in comparative organizational efficiencies the bigger the proportionate distances between the two curves. The further the MED curve from CC is, the larger is the 'minimum efficiency difference'.

Suppose, before continuing, we pause to consider how significant any differences between expected rates of return in this example would prove in practice. As a rough and ready 'reckoner' let us say that the capital project was to be enjoyed in perpetuity, and that annual payments took the form of an annuity, to be similarly enjoyed. In this case, the ratio of V_A to V_B would be equal to the ratio of r_B to r_A. For example, if the rate of return expected by consortium A was 10 per cent and by B was 5 per cent, then consortium B would be willing to commit *twice* the real resource today as A in exchange for the same future stream of payments to be guaranteed by the state; the proportionate difference would be 100 per cent; and the minimum efficiency difference curve MED would have twice the vertical height of the reference curve CC.[10] (We should perhaps emphasize that the example is chosen because the algebra in this stylized instance is easy to present – it is only an example: it flags up how potentially sensitive resource commitments might be to expected returns. But the use of Figure 4.1 and analysis thereof is completely general, vis-à-vis our subject).

Our interest, as we have said, in this thought experiment is by analogy. Suppose we were to take the commitments of the state to successful PFI consortiums – the stream of future payments to be awarded the private sector contract holders – as a base point of reference; and suppose we then ask how much *larger* the real resource commitment of the state towards investing in public services provision would have been at the outset, if the *same* money owing in the future had been borrowed on the *cheaper* terms possible were finance raised through long-term bond issues. Conversely, suppose we were to ask, again on an analogous basis, just how inefficient the state sector would have to be in organizational terms – given that the package deal driving the PFI policy links financing routes for project investment to project delivery – before it becomes possible to justify this more expensive route to financial provision. In asking this question, we take as granted, for the moment, the dual function of PFI (both to raise finance for capital projects, and to undertake to organize the investment). Evidently, a view of some sort is taken that the private sector can achieve more with less.

What is remarkable, however, is how big this difference would have to be if properly acknowledged based on the real returns expected on PFI contracts, which have often exceeded real post-tax rates of return on bond issues by *very* large margins. In an early estimate, Gaffney et al. (1999: 177) (also cited in Sawyer 2003: 177) suggest expected annual real rates of return for PFI in the region of 15 to 25 percent. The government's *own* estimate, covering the period 1995 to 2001, suggests that the 'all-in' cost of private finance fell to just under 10 per cent, from over 13 per cent (H.M. Treasury 2003: 123; cited by Sawyer 2005: 247). By contrast, and following Sawyer (2003), the real post-tax rate of return on bond issues for much of the life of these PFI initiatives has been as low as 2 ½ per cent. PFI contacts are awarded on capital projects with life spans of up to 25 to 30 years: and therefore relatively long lived. If we then ask how comparatively inefficient the state sector would have to be to justify electing to borrow over this kind of time frame at rates estimated at ranges from 10 per cent to upwards of 25 per cent on the one hand (PFI), rather than at 2 ½ per cent, the answer is that the posited difference in competence would be very big. In other words, if we think of the PFI initiative as a vehicle by which to gauge how deep an institutionalized assumption might go vis-à-vis the perceived inefficiency of public sector management relative to private, then it might go very deep indeed.

What the state does

One possible objection to this way of framing the question is that the long-term costs to the state of borrowing to fund investment from bond issues would certainly have been increased had this route to raising funds been preferred to the PFI, simply as a consequence of the cumulatively large size of the borrowing effort. It could then be argued that the figure Sawyer (2003) suggests of a real post-tax rate of return on bond issues of 2 ½ per cent for public sector finance is too low – because even at that time it would not have remained this low *had* the PFI policy been abandoned. But a moment's thought establishes that even if this is true so far as it goes,[11] for the issue at hand its merits are less clear: PFI contracts are awarded on a case-by-case basis, so that in every instance where a contract was awarded the relevant consideration in ascertaining the logic of *that* decision would be the extant return on bonds.

A more difficult issue is the way in which PFI contracts are actually awarded by the state, under Treasury rules governing these decisions.

Before a contract is awarded under the terms governing the policy a comparison is made between each private sector project proposal and a Public Sector Comparator (PSC). The manner in which this is done accounts in part for the frustrated tone of much of the critical literature, not least from public sector experts, aimed against the scheme.

In the first instance, our simple thought experiment, and our assessment so far of the issues raised by the PFI scheme vis-à-vis the public and private spheres, highlights a difference in the real rates of return expected by the private sector consortiums who win contracts under the Treasury-governed application of the scheme, and the real post-tax rates of return that would be required on government debt issues. What the rules actually employed do is to ignore these considerations: instead, a *single* discount rate is used to compare two expenditure profiles over time – the first the stream of future payments to the private sector for which the state would be liable were the private sector consortium successful in winning a PFI contract, and the second an estimated stream for the public sector against which to compare (the PSC). The discount rate employed to compare the two income streams is a real rate of discount, cast in constant price (inflation subtracted) terms (see Sawyer 2003: 178–80); it is known to be typically lower than the real rate of return actually expected by the private sector investors in PFI projects, but at the same time higher than the terms upon which public sector borrowing would have been possible. From our perspective, this means that the Treasury rules give an estimated value of the real resource commitment today of future taxpayers to public sector projects that may be far in excess of the actual amount which private consortiums intend to commit. The real rate of return that they expect from their investment being higher than the Treasury discount rate, the correspondingly smaller the sum that they intend to invest. At the same time, the same Treasury rules understate how much could be committed in real terms for the same set of state liabilities were these incurred in other ways.[12]

Critics have generally regarded this procedure as rigged. In the second instance, while the Treasury rules allow that payments to private sector firms for PFI should be treated as being spread out over the life of the contracts (often 25 to 30 years), it is assumed that for public sector organization all capital costs are incurred right at the outset. Thus while state borrowing through traditional routes is possible on a longer-term basis, the rules adopted by the Treasury elect to ignore this possibility. Furthermore, at the point of construction the Public Sector Comparator (PSC) is required to *build in* an assumption that its costs are likely to be higher than private sector costs. Quite remarkably, even with all of these assisting considerations vis-à-vis the rules which the Treasury requires of PFI awards, the decision is known to be often marginal – that is, it is still a close run thing (Sawyer 2003: 178–9) (citing hospital contracts discussed in Gaffney et al. 1999: see also Pollock and Price 2004).

However, the difficulty that this causes is an interesting one. The rules governing the bidding process for PFI contracts require that the public sector assume that it will suffer a cost disadvantage vis-à-vis the private sector, in the form of the built-in assumption that costs will be higher – to add to the PSC – for public management. We might think of this as the 'acknowledged' bias against the public sector. But we can identify a far more substantial bias against public sector management if we take the route identified in our thought experiment above, and ask what the minimum efficiency difference would have to be for the PFI route to borrowing to make sense if the same future liabilities had been incurred through bond issues. We might think of this as the 'unacknowledged' bias against public sector management, because the rules adopted by the Treasury acknowledge none of the relevant issues.

If we return then to our initial question and ask just how incompetent the state is assuming its own organs to be in organizing project delivery, then if differences in the costs of capital are explicitly recognized, the answer is *very* incompetent indeed. But the actual Treasury rules seem designed to understate the issue – claiming *some* comparative inefficiency at the level of public sector comparisons, but embedded in an approach that conceals a far greater and unacknowledged bias.

Risk transfers: nonsense and legitimation

It is of interest in this connection to consider the language of legitimation. For example, it is sometimes proposed that that the PFI scheme has the bonus feature of transferring risk from the public sector to the private sector, in the sense that with the government committed to a fixed stream of future payments to the contract holders, any cost overruns experienced by a private sector consortium on a project must be paid for out of its *own* future profits, *rather* than money *from* the state:

> The involvement of private finance in taking on risk is cru-cial.... Private finance in PFI, particularly third-party finance, takes the risks in a project and allocates them to the party best able to manage them. The lenders to a PFI project, as they have significant capital at risk, have a powerful incentive to identify, allocate and ensure the effective management of all the risks the private sector assumes. (H. M. Treasury 2003: 10; cited in Sawyer 2005: 240)

The same noises are made by admirers of the scheme like Anthony Giddens:

> The key question in evaluating PFI is whether or not risk is taken over sufficiently by the private sector ... critics are vociferous in claiming that it is an expensive means of funding public projects, since the government can borrow money more cheaply ... the com-parison made here is false ... PFI builds in the cost of risk. (Giddens 2002: 62)

But let us first recall that when a PFI contract is awarded to a private consortium by the state, the real rate of the return that the con-sortium expects on the investment it will make is the source both of its own anticipated profits and of the interest payments to the private sector investors who have supplied funds for the project. If from the viewpoint of these investors the project is deemed to be 'risky', this concern is already factored into the interest payments they will require on their loans. The return expected by the holders of the PFI contract includes any risk premium: if it is accepted, it is not accepted *gratis* because the state *pays* for it. And the implication of the way in which the state pays for it is that the higher this risk is believed to be, the *smaller* the real resource commitment which will be made on behalf of the public by the private sector in exchange for future taxpayers money. In this regard, it makes no more sense to describe the nominal transfer of risk to the private sector follow-ing the award of a PFI contract as a 'bonus' or 'extra' feature than it would to so describe the transfer of a tin of beans from a grocer to a customer in a corner shop after the customer hands over the money demanded for the exchange.

And insofar as the question of the assumption implicitly made about the comparative ineffectiveness of public sector management vis-à-vis the private, nothing alters. The view is still taken that with the smaller real resource commitment today the private sector will manage to deliver more than the public sector could with a larger – and again, the Treasury rules hide away the size of this assumption.[13]

It is perhaps worth noting in this connection that one of the major side disputes on the conduct and progress of the PFI policy have been windfall gains realized repeatedly by contract holders achieved via post-contract refinancing deals. As capital projects progress, it has been common for the private consortiums of firms organizing these projects to pay back loans to private investors in those schemes using money borrowed after the 'risky' phase – to realize a larger profit. If nothing else happens, then from the viewpoint of the consortium this is a windfall gain. It does not in any way alter the circumstances – the judgement of the state – at the point where the contract was awarded, but does redistribute the return to be made on the investment in the capital project with regard to different parts of the private sector. It is also not unreasonable to speculate – abandoning the 'no moral hazard' assumption made earlier in our illustrative thought experiment – on whether some consortiums deliberately seek out high interest backing from third-party financers at the start of the PFI process in order to obtain 'windfall' gains via refinancing deals later on.[14]

But on the issue of risk transfer, some scepticism is occasionally expressed as to whether having paid the private sector to 'accept' the risk being 'transferred' – and again we should observe a somewhat loaded use of the English language – the state would then actually allow PFI-funded schemes to fail because of cost overruns. It has been widely speculated that in practice private sector consortiums would attempt to renegotiate the terms of the original contract to win a more generous payment – or to withdraw while managing to leave some of their own liabilities with the state. Were contracts to be renegotiated so that extra assistance was given to private schemes, the situation could best be described as a 'soft budget', in which the fixed future streams of payments from the state turn out not to be fixed at all. If the initial award for the PFI contract were still to be justified – that in some sense the transfer of responsibilities to the private sector for capital project organization nonetheless reflected upon a balance of relative advantages – we could think of an upwards shift in the position of the MED curve in Figure 4.1 *ex post* compared to *ex ante*.

Implications and speculations

Earlier in this chapter we noted the seeming abruptness of the departure in public policy debate in the 1980s vis-à-vis the degree to which a predisposition emerged favouring private sector over public sector organization, and that after its election in 1997, the first government of Tony Blair quickly set about confirming that there would be no reversals of the privatizations of public sector enterprises. Moreover, there was no attempt to hide a predisposition towards a working assumption that private sector management *is* better management. In these contexts, we ask what can be made of the Private Finance Initiative (PFI), heavily developed and promoted under the leadership of ex-Chancellor Gordon Brown, under the terms of which the boundaries of the state at one level expand, while at the same time seeming to contract – a trick managed by the expedient of increasing the share of future tax revenues that will flow back into private sector coffers – as the involvement of privately owned businesses in the organization of the public sector increases. One main conclusion is that if the procedures of 'due diligence' laid down by the relevant government department (the UK Treasury) in governing the award of contracts for major capital investment projects make free use of the assumption that were work to remain in the public sector there would be cost overruns, these procedures themselves mask – to potentially very substantive effect – a much larger predisposition right from the outset to favour the private over the public.

In the early days of the New Labour project, and as it became apparent that the new Labour government intended to apply itself accordingly, supporters were apt to argue that previous policy dispensations had tended to confuse means with ends. The 'real problem', according to Tony Wright (1997: 26), was not nationalization as such, but rather the implied, and 'classic', 'confusion of means and ends' – 'Politics are for changing, as circumstances and problems change. Values are for keeping, as the enduring reference point by which policy compasses are set' (ibid.) (the same passage is also cited and discussed further in Driver and Martell (1998: 26)). As a theory of nationalization, or for that matter of any kind of state organization of the economy, this leaves a lot to be desired. The prognosis that the long swing towards an increasingly public economy described by Florio (2004) – also briefly touched upon in the opening parts of this chapter – reflected simply a century or so of confusion between means and ends hardly appeals to historical reflection.

But the means and ends distinction is an interesting one; because whenever pushed on the *means* by which public sector investment in Britain is now managed, far from showing any keenness to expound on the rationalities of the process, a stock response – especially from government ministers – has been to emphasize *ends*: 'If we retreat from PFI', Gordon Brown told the *Guardian* newspaper ahead of his defence of PFI to a sceptical Labour Party conference, 'and still say that schools and hospitals still have to be built, we will end up with the old quick fixes and retreat into unsustainable borrowing' (cited in Coates 2005c: 69). The quote admittedly blurs the two, but if we disregard the last part of Brown's defence as the effort of someone not prepared to concede that the PFI policy is public sector borrowing – a concession freely admitted to even by Anthony Giddens, an admirer (see Giddens 2002: 62) – the first part has proved to be remarkably effective in keeping a lid on wider unease. At the very least, New Labour *would* build and refurbish schools, *would* build and refurbish hospitals, and *would* upgrade parts of the crumbling public infrastructure.

It is unlikely in the extreme that the Treasury or any current government minister would be willing to describe the Treasury rules governing PFI as an embodied reflection of an unacknowledged bias against the state sector, and one certainly much larger than the biases which are happily admitted to. Allyson Pollock, a critic not only of private financing but of a number of other reforms impacting on the NHS, notes how when asked by one minister to explain her concerns, he 'responded by praising the virtues of the private sector and inviting me to join him for a drink'; Gordon Brown is said to have responded by declaring 'repeatedly', 'that the public sector is bad at management, and that only the private sector is efficient' (Pollock et al. 2005: 3). The general import of the PFI is that it provides a window into how this belief emerges not only *within* the terms allowed by institutional processes, but also how deep it might go when explaining their elisions: the self-effacing state may also be self-deceiving.

In any case, and while a point briefly and easily made it is one which should be given an appropriately heavy weighting, there is very little that can be identified in terms of empirical evidence which would imply that the privatizations undertaken before Tony Blair and Gordon Brown – first by Mrs Thatcher's governments and then by John Major's – actually did anything to improve the efficiencies with which the assets in question were actually utilized. There are, of course, some major difficulties involved when comparing public and private organizations, even when considering the effects of privatization on previously public enterprises producing marketed goods or services – sold with 'prices' attached. But where there is felt to be sufficient points of agreement for intelligible comparisons between previously public enterprises in Britain rendered private (typically hedged around with multiple qualifications and interpretative guesswork), all that is clear, for example, on questions of 'productivity' is that the case for privatization cannot easily be justified in retrospect: for instance, by studies of the public sector enterprises privatized by Mrs Thatcher.[15] And where cost reductions have been achieved by privatizations – or by previous experiments in the outsourcing of public services to the private sector – the balance of evidence suggests a major downwards pressure on terms and conditions of employment.

What is not in doubt, however, are the massive distributional impacts that were entailed by Mrs Thatcher's privatizations, the reduction in the net worth of the state as these assets were sold below value – generating easy sales and windfall gains for the buyers of the share issues, but providing less revenue to the state that the capitalized value of future net earnings would have afforded – as well as the changing price and provision policies of some of the privatized entities. Broadly speaking, it is not illegitimate to say that the distributional losers were the larger part of the UK population (judged on a relative headcount) – taxpayers generally, and at many junctures consumers, including pensioners and families on lower incomes.[16] The major feature of the PFI policy scheme over the longer term is likewise likely to be deemed to be a regressively redistributional one, in a context delineated by a far smaller accumulation of capital assets designated for public services provision than would have been possible had borrowing been undertaken by traditional routes.[17]

Summing up

We commenced this chapter by suggesting that the Private Finance Initiative – or PFI – by its conception and implementation has the potential to offer insight into just how deeply an assumption of private sector efficacy runs though UK state policy. The expansion of PFI-like initiatives around the world, with Britain carrying on in the demonstrative tradition of Mrs Thatcher, points to an avenue for comparative research, focusing again on the potential for investigating, via careful scrutiny of processes and outcomes, the degrees of pro-market biases shown in other experiments. What is of particular, and still largely unexplored relevance, is that the bias against public sector management of public sector services provision acknowledged *within* the terms of the rules governing the award of PFI contracts is in all likelihood small when compared with any 'guesstimate' of the unacknowledged bias *hidden* behind these rules. This is a problem for sociology and political science – as much as public sector administration or bookkeeping – to explore. There is an ostensible rationality at play that nonetheless hides away the enormity of its own assumptions; and at the same time, the defence that means must not be confused with ends is oddly inverted.

In tracing out the contrary demands of modernization after Mrs Thatcher vis-à-vis an expanded public services provision, but within a pro-private sector dispensation, it may be possible to better understand the contradictions engendered by the squared circle of an *expanding* state presence but a *shrinking* state organization – realisable only at the expense of funnelling money on more expensive terms to the private sector, and 'squared away' at the expense of a self-deceiving as much as a self-effacing posture. At the same time, the result is not quite Thatcherism – although longer-term regressive and redistributive consequences are apparent. As a window into the state under New Labour, and of the consequences of squaring away contrary pressures, there is much to be obtained by reflecting upon its expansively humble character.

5
The Self-Deceiving State: The 'Model Employer' Myth

It is a fondly held belief internationally that the state sector, and whatever its other shortcomings, is at least a 'model employer' or preferential employer for state workers. In countries where the state sector is large – and two of the largest individual employers in Western Europe are UK state sectors – this is a substantial assumption which has influenced the characterization and analysis of the more general behaviour of the state in recent decades. If the study of the UK Private Finance Initiative in the previous chapter suggests an almost alarming degree of modesty is possible on the part of nation states with respect to their own capabilities, then their alacrity to claim 'model employer' status also requires critical academic engagement. Quite generally, we are faced here with an apparent paradox: the liberalization of public services, fuelled by private sector interests through a panoply of international institutions (not least the World Trade Organization through the General Agreement on Trade in Services),[1] has been a global phenomenon with increasing reach and depth and involves inter alia the transfer of workers from public *to* private sector employment. At the same time, the capacity of states across the globe to characterize themselves as model employers with respect to their own workers (a large and growing proportion of whom are women) suggests a deficit *in* private sector employment practice which should warn *against* liberalization.

It is clearly important to explore the tensions visible here between state conceptions of 'efficiency', on the one hand, and 'equity' on the other. In this chapter, we begin with an assessment of the conceptual roots for the idea of 'model employer' and its prevalent usages internationally, and not least as applied to states; an important preliminary step if the significance of this tension – not only in Britain but also more globally – is to be properly understood. Then, and using the United Kingdom as a prime example, and with a keen eye on gender, we note the particular development of this concept, alongside the rather mixed evidence, historically and currently, on how the state actually discharges its obligations to its own workforce. We locate this discussion finally in a consideration of policies under New Labour, and how this in turn reflects upon state attitudes towards issues of wider labour market deregulation.

We fundamentally revise how the UK state is typically regarded in these connections. A more complex picture emerges, in which the term 'model employer' is a nuanced one and where the state's own cost imperative with regard to its employees acts as a tacit constraint on policies adopted more generally, moderated by the degree of pressure produced by trade unions. In addition, we see more particularly that the UK state sector fares very badly in any assessment of gender segregation at work and of low or unequal pay for women. We thereby challenge any general precept that the state *is* a model employer in a simple descriptive sense, highlighting the internal tensions between the rhetoric of policy objectives involving equity and the reality of policies focused on short-term cost economies, which segue into wider policy tensions and impediments to improvements in the position of workers – and women workers – in the economy as a whole. At the same time, we explore whether an apparent degree of self-deception on the part of states can be understood through the lens of legitimation, thus squaring to some extent the seeming paradox between concurrent rhetoric of liberalization and model employment. One point needs to be stressed from the outset: an historically framed approach to the issues explored in this chapter identifies cyclical stresses overlaying long stretches of continuity in main aspects of state employment, essential to a proper understanding both of the limits of Thatcherism – its dramatic effects elsewhere notwithstanding – and of the inheritance of New Labour.

Rooting out the myth

As H.G. Wells famously noted, once people have repeated a phrase a great number of times, they begin to realize it has meaning and may even be true. In a sense, our framing principle is to ask: does 'model employer' have meaning, and is it true? The concept of model employer has a long history across different sectors and models of the economy. The term can often be found applied to the early philanthropic ideas of the British cotton mill owner and reformer, Robert Owen (1771–1858), and his New Harmony model cooperative community experiment.[2]

The term has also been used in the context of private sector firms' own claims to relative generosity of treatment of their employees, and to coverage of 'good' or 'model' employer practices by private firms in the business press. This kind of usage is longstanding and geographically widespread. The concept is one in fact which extends well beyond usages within advanced industrial countries.[3] A sophisticated theoretical and empirical literature has developed in the context of US business, exploring historical trends in management rhetoric (for example, Barley and Kunda 1992; Abrahamson 1997; and Shenhav 1999). For Barley and Kunda (1992), management discourse swings between two poles of 'normative' and 'rational' control: *normative* control highlights 'winning hearts and minds' as a key to achieving higher worker morale and productivity through the subtle exercise of 'moral authority', while *rational* control emphasizes the systematized deployment of labour as a (self-interested) factor of production in the most efficient combination with other 'factors' (ibid.: 364). We might also understand these terms more generally, for the purposes of this chapter's exploration, as those controls emphasizing an employer's normative (or beneficent) aspirations for employees with those explicitly addressing what it considers its own rational needs or efficiency requirements. Each may have legitimizing aspects.

These themes are further developed by Haydu and Lee (2004), who in an important study compare business press profiling of model employers in the last two decades of the twentieth century (1980–1999) with profiling in the last two decades of the nineteenth century (1880–1899). While broadly supporting Barley and Kunda in their 'more general characterization of management rhetoric in the two eras as favouring "normative" control' (2004: 183) they find that that 'in both periods, the business press's model employer is nearly as concerned with rationalizing work as he is with cultivating employee needs' (2004: 184). They identify a 'stark difference' in conceptions of *which* specific employment practices were deemed most likely to improve 'efficiency' – 'what more rational management actually *meant*' (ibid.: 185): interestingly, they find that while the nineteenth-century good employer sought to make work more bureaucratic, the twentieth-century counterpart sought to make it less so. And they go on to argue that both the 'distinctive features' and 'substance' of each period's model employer – as profiled in the business press – mirrored contemporary 'currents in political reform' (ibid.: 188), as well as the concerns of the day: social unrest in the nineteenth century, and national decline in the 20th. They infer, for example, similarities between the discourse of Ronald Reagan's backlash against 'liberalism' – calls for deregulation, decentralization, and unfettered markets and competition (ibid.: 195) – and the encouragement of individual entrepreneurship, flexibility, and self-interest on the part of employees, as featured in lists of employers' virtues in the business press of the late twentieth century. We can note that the *language* of this later era, especially 'flexibility', is also reflected in what we will find for the United Kingdom.

While past and present usages in the cooperative and private sectors suggest important themes for analysis, our subject matter in this chapter is the predominant usage of the term in the political sphere with reference to *government* as employer. This usage is found across the globe, most particularly in advanced or developing industrialized economies with developed or developing welfare states. Here too, normative preoccupations have tended to dominate, with claims to generosity and fairness – or aspirations for this – being made by governments themselves, or those commenting on them; and alongside notions that the state – will or should – set an example *to* the private sector. However, rational preoccupations can also be seen, along with some degree of a shift towards an emphasis on 'flexibilities'.

In the United States, for example, and with a wide-ranging accompanying set of proposals for new employment practice, Theodore Roosevelt proclaimed in his State of the Union address of 3 December 1907 that 'the National Government should be a model employer' demanding 'the highest quality of service from each of its employees' and caring 'for all of them properly in return'. Lyndon B. Johnson took this assumed ideal of 'reciprocity' of obligations further in his statement of 7 March 1966, which overtly encompassed issues of efficiency and cost reduction:

> The Federal government is the largest employer in the nation. The largest employer has an undeniable responsibility to lead, and not

merely to follow, in instituting and adhering to model employment practices. A model employer can demand excellence in performance. A model employer can demand continuing awareness
of the need for greater productivity, more imaginative conduct of
Government programs, and substantial cost reduction.

More recently, the term has been employed, generally in its more normative and exhortatory connotations, by President Bill Clinton on
making the federal government a model employer to set the example
in the area of child support enforcement,[4] and by Al Gore.[5] The term
was also widely applied in coverage of the disabilities initiatives by
both President Bushes.[6] Most recently, it has been used by Hillary
Clinton in a press release for her election campaign with respect to
paid parental leave (16 October 2007). And its prevalence remains high
in the United States. References can be found in current websites for:
Time; the Office of Disability Employment Policy; Labor and Defense
Department; National Guard and Reserve Employees; United States
Federal Government (USA JOBS); Congressional Budget Office (regarding retirement payments); US Patent and Trademark office; and on
numerous state websites. Moreover, a very influential lead on usage of
the term in the United States has recently been given by the US Equal
Employment Opportunity Commission (August 2007): 'As a model
employer, federal agencies must set an example that all other employers, public and private, can look to as a positive example ... [embodying]
the concepts of fairness, inclusion and diversity'.[7]

Recent and current references to government as a model employer
can also be found across the globe: in India (Government Pay
Commission); in Canada (Government Human Resources and Social
Development, with reference to model employment of people with
disabilities); in the Caribbean (Caribbean Enterprise Forum); in Fiji; in
Australia (Human Rights and Equal Opportunity Commission with
respect to Australian Public Service and disability/employment); in
South Africa (Gauteng Provincial Government); in Sweden; in Malta;
in Pakistan (Minister for Social Welfare and Special Education with
respect to workers with disabilities); in South East Asia; and even in
commentary on the evolving CEE countries (Open Society Institute –
George Soros).

If the geographical spread and importance of this term at the most
senior levels of government, as well as on the part of third-party

commentators, is certain, its meaning is rather less so. It can be seen from the selective coverage above that there has tended to be a spectrum running from the normative to the rational. While normative usages tend to predominate, these are more often aspirational or exhortatory rather than direct claims to be a model employer in practice – although these latter claims are sometimes made – and rational arguments sometimes lurk within them. To explore this spectrum further we turn to the usage in the United Kingdom of the terminology of government as model employer, which is also currently seeing something of a renaissance.

Modern usage in the United Kingdom

Recent academic analysis of the modern forms of the government as model employer in the United Kingdom has tended to emphasize top-down institutional arrangements and effects on industrial peace, for example by signalling departures from prior 'golden age' arrangements arising from dated breaks in the wider political and industrial relations arena. They have also tended to conflate 'normative' (or 'rational') claims with empirical substance. An older tradition, for example Wootton (1955), Clegg and Chester (1957), and Harvey and Hood (1958), took a more circumspect view of the state and conditions of employment within it than more recent efforts, and here undoubtedly it is possible to see a reaction to the Conservative administrations from 1979. In the next section, we will make the case for a similarly deliberative approach; but first we provide some indicative sense of recent usages in the United Kingdom of the model employer construct.

The recent usage is evident in the influential work of Fredman and Morris (1989a, b), where the concept is given strong normative connotations and focused around several key themes. Firstly, it is argued that 'an important aspect of the State in its role as employer was its desire to set an example to the private sector...indeed, this was one of the primary motivations for the introduction of collective bargaining into the civil service in 1919' (1989a: 10). Secondly, despite noting some problems with the 'model good employer ideal' in terms of pay outcomes in parts of the public sector, it is argued that the ideal 'remained a central part of the ideology of successive governments until 1979' (ibid.: 11), with encouragement of trade union organization, commitment to collective bargaining, and a high degree of job security offered (ibid.: 1). The decade from 1979 is then contrasted as representing a transformation of the role of the state as employer, with the direction of influence reversed and the government attempting to 'apply private-sector, free-market ideas to its own employment practices' (ibid.). The argument here is that the government's attitude 'changed radically', becoming 'increasingly opposed to industry-wide collective bargaining' and placing more emphasis upon market forces and individual performance than on the criterion of 'comparability' which was previously 'the primary principle, combined with the desire to be a generally "good" employer' (ibid.: 142–3).

Variants on this approach are routinely found in textbook approaches. Farnham and Pimlott argue, for example, that

> By the late 1970s, the position of the government as a model employer was generally acknowledged. The government's chief characteristics as a model employer were: the automatic recognition of the right of trade unions to represent the government's employees; the acceptance of collective bargaining – largely at national level – for the determination of pay and conditions of employment; and the wide-spread use of joint consultation procedures... Considerable efforts were also made in the period 1945 to 1979, to ensure that the pay of public sector employees was broadly comparable with that of the private sector. The general election of 1979, however, marked a clear change in the attitude of government to this role of model employer. (1995: 213)

Disjuncture theories, often emphasizing a break from 1979 with the election of Mrs Thatcher, and built around the notion of a previously model employer, are found in the most erudite of public sector studies, even where there is a detailed historical and analytical approach, and even when different periodizations and definitions are employed.[8] For example, Farnham, Horton, and Giles (1994) whilst qualifying the roles of 'model' and 'good practice' employer with the 'differing shades of meaning' attaching to these ideas over time, and to a growing understanding that such practices did not necessarily constitute an obligation by the state to offer the highest rates of pay, nonetheless still stress:

> the distinctive role of public organizations as *benevolent employers*, with 'model' and 'good' employment practices... As model, good

practice employers, the public sector aimed to provide terms and
conditions, and ways of determining them, which would act as
examples for other, mainly private employers to follow. Public
employers also wanted, on the grounds of comparability, to provide, where necessary, terms and conditions in line with those of
the best companies. (1994: 7; emphasis in original)

By characterizing the government's role in public sector industrial relations in this way, these authors are then still able to debate
whether a 'hybrid' model of public sector personnel management
has been emerging since 1979 (ibid.: 2).

Even in recent accounts based on a more explicit acknowledgement of the existence of divergent interest groups and the importance of substantive outcomes in terms of pay and conditions of
work, the 'ghost' of the concept of model employer lingers on, as
for example, in the work of Carter and Fairbrother (1999). Here, as
Bach (1999) puts it with respect to these writers, the authors 'suggest
that there was no golden era of public-service industrial relations,
but acknowledge that aspects of the "model employer" philosophy
did prevail, albeit in partial and uneven forms' (ibid.: 100). Thus in
this contribution too, as well as in Bach's reading of it, the possibility
of a variant on the disjuncture thesis is left more than a little open.
A discontinuity is again traced from the early 1980s: 'the state's role
as an employer' was at this point 'thrown into sharp relief, – 'broadly
changing' from one 'aspiring to "model employer" status' to one
'attempting to model itself on "best" private-sector practice' (Carter
and Fairbrother 1999: 119; following Fredman and Morris 1989b).
It is argued that there has been a shift from the 'relatively opaque
employment relations' under the 'model employer' era to one where
'relations between management and employees have become more
transparent as waged relationships' (1999: 122).

In a circumspect and important contribution, Morgan and
Allington (2002) again pose the question '[h]as the public sector retained its "model employer" status' – and again taking as
their comparison the situation as it existed 'before the late 1970s'
(ibid.: 35). While continuing the trend noted above towards formulation of a disjuncture theory, and an acceptance of the relevance of
'model employer' terminology prior to 1979, these authors nonetheless provide a careful comparison of private and public sector HRM

practices, including job security, flexible working, temporary and fixed-term contracts, trade union membership, collective bargaining, equal employment opportunities, and public versus private sector pay. They conclude that the 'hard' model of HRM appeared to be winning out over the 'soft' model in at least three major areas: job restructuring, protective trade union legislation, and public sector pay (ibid.: 40).

While some concessions have been made by its proponents in other work,[9] and despite the nuances of the analysis above by Morgan and Allington, it is fair to say that the benign model employer perspective survives in its broad essentials as a starting point for accounts of state sector employment: as, for example, in Bach and Winchester (2003: 287). Moreover, since the election of a Labour government in 1997, the precise status of New Labour within this tradition remains as yet unsettled in the literature. Notwithstanding concerns over Thatcherism, the view taken on the relative position of public sector workers vis-à-vis their private sector counterparts is very positive: 'many public sector workers enjoy relatively high job security, shorter working hours... while low pay is also relatively rare' (Bach and Winchester, 2003: 286). Gender disadvantage is acknowledged, but again the prognosis is optimistic: 'in most parts of the public services... the gender pay gap and other expressions of women's disadvantaged position vis-à-vis men have declined over the last 20 years' (ibid.: 294–5). This is explained in part on the basis of the impetus given by recruitment and retention difficulties; and it is argued more generally that public sector employers have responded 'more positively than their private service counterparts' to the pressure from trade unions and employment tribunal decisions in seeking to develop equal opportunities policies (ibid.: 294–5). The state, however, remains a prime mover and the perspectives adopted in narratives of this kind – the most common approach – tend to be top down.

A recent renaissance of the use of the model employer terminology by government in Britain (including New Labour) – as in the United States and other countries internationally – is likely to fuel the need for rigorous academic analysis of the concept. In one of the furthest ranging arguments, exhibiting both 'normative' and 'rational' preoccupations in the senses described previously – and with some interesting mirrors of the changing emphasis given to rational accounts as per Haydu and Lee above – the UK Department of Health's policy guidance currently makes 'the case for becoming a model employer' as follows:

> There is a wealth of research evidence which demonstrates clear links between good employment practices and business outcomes. Creating an environment where staff are valued, rewarded, appropriately trained and developed, regularly appraised and properly managed has a positive impact on people who use services and their carers. Model employers are also more likely to attract and retain high-quality staff and are also more likely to have high-performing and motivated staff who are more flexible and take less time off work.
>
> For social care, *People need People* – the report on the outcomes of the joint Social Services Inspectorate and Audit Commission inspections (2000), found that: 'Those councils that are performing best in service delivery and the management of performance and resources are also those who score highly on their management of workers.'[10]

This guidance goes on to argue that 'being a model employer means developing and implementing the right people management practices for your workforce', with such practices covering a wide range of issues including 'good benefits including reward structures and leave allowances' as well as 'progressive policies on diversity' (ibid.). The model employer concept was previously included in the NHS Plan in July 2000, and subsequently in new pay systems in the NHS in the 2000s. Self-references – self-descriptions – as model employers can now be found widely on websites and in internal documentation for health service trusts, and also for local authorities in the United Kingdom.

There is therefore likely to be a renewed interest by academics both in decomposing the term and in applying a judgement to the New Labour government post-1997 (as well as in exploring this usage internationally, and for the private sector). Early signs of this interest in the United Kingdom can be seen. For example, in a recent paper exploring Anglo-American ideals of the model employer in the private sector, Gibb (2004) coherently argues that there may be multiple models exhibiting tensions between social and organizational understandings and between 'subjective perceptions and concerns of differing groups with different interests' (ibid.: 294). Interestingly, for Gibb it is the analysis of the social construction of the concept and its *symbolic* usage or 'legitimacy' that is of more interest than 'integrating themes or winnowing out the valid factors'; he concludes by arguing for the 'acceptance of a plurality of models, treated with equal legitimacy and equal measures of scepticism' (ibid.: 294–5). By contrast, in an interesting and unusual paper, Fielden and Whiting seek to provide substance to the concept as employed in the NHS through precisely an *empirical* exploration of employees' understanding of the 'psychological contract' and an evaluation of 'model employment' by contrasting the importance attached to a range of items by employees with their satisfaction levels (2006: 94–104).

It is clear that there is the potential for a very wide variety of academic interpretations of both the concept and the usage of the term 'model employer'. Analyses in the private sector have somewhat paradoxically, overall tended to be more subtle and complex than those dominating public sector accounts. With this in mind, we turn to a reappraisal of the concept, using illustrative example from the UK public sector.

The myth explored: challenges to orthodoxy

The global prevalence of references to the 'model employer', both within and without the public sector, and the shifting and nuanced shades of meaning attaching to it, suggest that when assessing the particular experience of the United Kingdom a clear evaluation is needed of its specific features – historical as well as current – if we are to draw out the implications of this experience for the interpretation of evolving British state policy in practice. Moreover, a longer view is needed if an adequate sense is to be had of the importance of the cyclical stresses overlaying continuities referred to in the introduction to this chapter. Some general observations in this regard may be helpful. It is obviously important not to conflate mythology with actual practice, otherwise artificial points of departure for analysis will tend to be produced (and reproduced), a problem with many recent attempts to theorize the 'model employer' state in a priori terms. Moreover, by casting the state and relations with its employees in an overly idealized context, this kind of analysis is in danger of offering little as regards causation and change.

In this section we build on an earlier tradition, acknowledging the importance of pressures 'from below' in determining change with regard to the role of organized labour and shifts and asymmetries in power over time, and developing a quite different perspective on the 'model employer' as this term might apply to the British state. In this context we also emphasize the importance of material outcomes (for example, wages), as well as procedures or processes, for an understanding of the state as an employer. To borrow a phrase from a different context, we must avoid evaluating 'procedural rights' above 'substantive interests' and outcomes (Hyman, 1989: 81). Conventional approaches tend to neglect the latter – making them prey to government as it presents itself. We emphasize the real conflicts, past and present, within the public sector, and their material causes in problems of low and unequal pay. We note the concomitant instability of institutional arrangements, and the nuanced and cyclically variable usage and meanings attached to terms like 'model employer' and 'fairness' or 'comparability'.

We organize the remainder of this section in three historical phases: a necessary convenience if we are to obtain an appropriately nuanced historical understanding of the changing development of the concept of the state as a model employer. We should note for non-specialists that state employment can be viewed as covering direct employment by the government (national and local) and employment of contract workers by government departments; and throughout there is also the issue of legislative 'encouragement' to the private sector in employment practice. In all of these roles, the key point of observation is that the government may be seen to have been, at best, reluctant in its concessions, more properly understood as driven by changes in trade union membership and militancy, and associated changes in the economic and global environment (including war).

Pressures from below: before the Great War

That the concept of the 'model' or 'good' employer ideal for the state sector was already well established can be seen in early debates about labour practice on government contracts. On the 13th February 1891, Sidney Buxton M.P. raised a motion in the House of Commons on this issue, asking that 'the State as a capitalist and employer should set a good example'. This gave rise to the Fair Wages Clause – and before the government conceded collective bargaining rights to its own employees (Allen, 1960: 88–9). But at the same time, scepticism about state employment practices was deeply felt. Thus when the

Webbs were writing in 1897, they saw the imperative of the government as little different from that of the 'profit-maker' in its 'permanent bias ... to lower the expense of production' (Webb and Webb 1897: 819). They flagged, however, particular power disparities between the state and its employees; the issue for the Webbs was therefore that of marshalling 'democratic public opinion' to influence the 'condition of Government employment' (ibid.: 554–5). They noted that 'trade union influence is, in spite of appearances, extremely ineffective ... unable to make its political power felt in Parliament' (ibid.). Thus, in another early reference to the concept of model employer, the Webbs argued that rhetoric did not necessarily reflect reality:

> It is in vain that Ministry after Ministry avows its intention of abandoning competition wages, and of making the Government a 'model employer' ... a trade union secretary will often declare that the Government, instead of being the best, is one of the very worst employers with whom he has to deal. (ibid.: 555)

Somewhat later, Phelps Brown (1959: 188) noted the relative lack of overt government concern about formal systems of industrial relations until the 1890s: it was only with the growth of New Unionism in the 1890s – the first emergence of a mass union membership outside of the existing craft structures – that government's role began to change (see ibid.: 358–60). Disputes in rail and coal in particular, prior to the First World War, suggested that the threat of industry-wide strikes was a determining factor (ibid.: 342–3). Governments also began to be confronted by trade unionism in the civil service; for example, trade unions first appeared in the Post Office, then the largest government department, from 1881. The state's reluctance in its role as model employer may be gauged from the fact that, despite according legal recognition to unions in 1871, 'the Government opposed the attempts of the postmen to form unions for some years afterwards', and the first recognition and agreement to negotiate only took place in 1906 (Allen 1960: 71–2).

The state's equally reluctant role in encouraging the adoption of 'fair' wages, particularly in government employment or contracts, can be seen in the early progress of Fair Wages Resolutions which also established standards for the wages and conditions of direct government employees (see especially Bercusson 1978). Again, it took an 'extraordinary eruption of industrial militancy' and the de facto emergence of collective bargaining and trade union strength to obtain the 1891 Resolution (1978: 11–16), a resolution subsequently dogged by problems of interpretation and intransigence on the part of local authorities and government departments (ibid.: 15–32). The situation was only somewhat ameliorated by increased political representation of Labour in Parliament, and the subsequently more sympathetic attitude of the Liberal party (ibid.: 112). Government's self-interest in cost control and market prices remained and, as noted by the Webbs above, a major factor (ibid.: 31). Replying to a complaint of low wages some eleven years after the Resolution was passed, the Financial Secretary to the War Office (in 1902), for example, claimed that:

> As a Government, we have to look at these matters as if we were managers of a business on behalf of the country, and to see that we do not set up a standard which will end, although there is a pecuniary advantage to the labourers, in a loss to the State. In all these matters our object must be to get the cheapest material and the cheapest form of labour combined, as it must be, in both cases, with the best class of material and the best form of labour. (ibid.: 79)

Even after the later 1909 Fair Wages Resolution, whether 'fair' wages should be interpreted as a current 'market' rate, current 'trade union' rate, or current 'best' rate, and for which particular market level, were questions remaining unresolved. In the end, it was left again to trade unions to complain, and unorganized workers were left unprotected. Thus, in this area as in others, 'as the resort to government departments for redress proved to be unavailing, trade unions and workers turned to the only means available to them – industrial warfare' (Bercusson 1978: 106). In this period, the 'model employer' might be invoked as a plea, with scepticism, or with irony – the pressure for change was from below, and with state concessions forced.

Pressures from below: war, depression, and Whitley

For later industrial relations writers and historians, and across the broadly defined range of activities for which the government would later be considered a bona-fide candidate for 'model employer', it was the First World War which combined with the steadily growing role and apparatus of the state to create a change in all the above circumstances, and force a new role for government. This period giving rise to, for example, the Whitley reports, which led to the establishment of joint industrial councils for national-level collective bargaining across a range of industries – the 'Whitley system' eventually becoming the main public sector pay determination system – is an important one for proponents of the model employer thesis (see, for example, Farnham & Pimlott, 1995: 212–3). However, a critical evaluation of the circumstances of the times leaves considerable scope for doubt as to whether the nature or extent of government's role had changed irrevocably, or for the good.

The years immediately before the First World War were characterized by industrial conflict, described by G.D.H. Cole as 'a mass movement of sheer reaction against the failure of either orthodox trade unionism or modern parliamentarianism to secure any improvement in the working class standard of life' (in Pelling 1968: 148). These years saw great increases in union membership and industrial disputes, alongside rises in the cost of living and relatively low levels of unemployment (Bercusson 1978: 121). At times of rising inflation, workers also became more insistent upon the criteria of relativity and comparability: '[w]hen war came the impulses towards combination were strengthened and the restraints removed' (Phelps Brown 1959: 360–1). Trade union membership doubled in five years, and the de facto growth of industry-wide bargaining and use of arbitration in this period laid the foundations for the Whitley Committee. That Whitley built upon existing arrangements and was forced through by the exigencies of industrial militancy – particularly unofficial disputes – in wartime (see also Clay 1929: 144–5; Bayliss 1962: 13; McCarthy & Clifford 1966: 39) is a strong qualification on suggestions that government had independently adopted a new role as model employer, although the government certainly took on board the idea that 'recourse to strike action is likely to lead to a widespread demand on the part of the public that "something should be done"', setting up Industrial Courts of Inquiry (the 1919 Act) to 'reassure people that this is, in fact, just what is happening' (McCarthy & Clifford 1966: 44). It also left some scope for doubt as to whether this new role would persist after the war.

The nature of the Whitley reports, and the efficacy of the ensuing system, has also been criticized. Clay (1929) noted that, in effect, wage earners were 'as dependent as before upon their own exertions and the strength of their own organizations to enforce their claims' (ibid.: 150–2). The Depression then 'rolled back' many of the 'advances' made by Whitley, such as they were (see Allen 1960: 63; Clay: 1929: 155–63; Bercusson 1978: 127–8; Bayliss 1962: 13–43). It was argued in a 1923 TUC/Labour Party pamphlet to be part of the 'consistent policy of employers to invoke either State or joint machinery for fixing wages, at a time when Labour is in a strong bargaining position', and to 'repudiate and abandon "all such interference" at a time when Labour is comparatively weak' (in Bercusson 1978: 127). Improvements made in the enforcement of the Fair Wages Resolutions at the start of the First World War were also eroded: the conflicting positions of the government had again been revealed in a 1918 discussion of amendments (ibid.: 140–56). That government took little further action until the 1930s led to growing concern at the extent of unemployment and unrest, and pressure from the TUC for reforms. A Fair Wages Committee in 1937–1939 was established as a holding operation (whose terms expressly excluded the consideration of wages policy for government employees), and little progress was made until the Second World War (ibid.: 168–227). Thus, in general, 'as the trade recession intensified so … the idealism which the Whitley Report … inspired receded and disappeared' (Allen 1960: 62–3) – and was 'swept away with unbelievable speed' (Bayliss 1962: 54). The big trade union membership losses sustained from 1921, until a slow resurgence in 1934, were 'accompanied by equally disastrous defeats over the maintenance of wages and conditions won during the war years' (Bercusson 1978: 130). The government in this situation adhered to a policy of leaving the parties to an industrial dispute to resolve their differences unaided. As Allen (1960) notes, 'it did not initiate additional measures to conciliate over-powerful employers' (ibid.: 64).

However, Whitley did seem to have particular, somewhat longer-term, significance for direct state employment; but it was the unions themselves who pressed for reform, and central and local government were resistant. By the First World War, trade unionism in the civil service was widespread if not very effective: war altered the service's character, with an influx of female and temporary workers; and at the end of the war ex-service men returned to their posts 'in a state of high expectancy' and ready to join trade unions (Allen 1960: 73).

Allen (ibid.) suggests that full recognition of their right to bargain col-
lectively was an 'inevitable outcome of this situation', only assisted by
Whitley whose recommendations had not in fact been intended for
the civil service. Government initially resisted the civil service unions'
proposals: but a concession was made in 1918 when the Cabinet
accepted modified proposals for government industrial workers and
then in 1919, after clerical civil servants 'became militant' and 'even
talked of strike action' (Humphreys cited in Allen 1960: 74), a government committee reported on the application of Whitley to administrative departments. It initially tried to exclude the determination of
wages, but eventually relented on this. The importance of distinguishing process from material outcomes here becomes very important.
As Allen noted, some problems could not be solved by the Whitley
system, not least the temptation for government to use the civil service 'as an easy way of cutting its expenditure', despite the best efforts
of the trade unions to maintain a vigilance against the government
departing from a role as model employer, and giving immediate publicity to any acts which did (Allen 1960: 73–83).

With respect to the *legitimizing* role of the concept of 'model
employer' and usage of 'comparability', as Clegg (1967) pointed out:

> Since the ability of the Treasury to meet increased pay and
> improvements in conditions is limited only by its ability to raise
> taxes, the official side requires some other criterion for its deci-
> sions than mere ability to pay. On the other hand the Treasury
> has in the past been peculiarly vulnerable to charges of niggardli-
> ness. Complaints on this score can receive wide publicity through
> parliamentary questions and debate, and the government of the
> day can afford even less than private firms to have the reputation
> of a bad employer. For this reason, some defence is needed. In the
> nineteenth century ministers and committees talked in terms of
> the wages necessary to secure an adequate supply of competent
> labour, and laid great weight on evidence concerning wages in
> comparable occupations outside the service. (ibid.: 238)

Indeed, comparability was a problematic concept and raised questions at the least about who sets the pay rates and round (Clegg
1967). Nonetheless, the principle of 'fair relativity' was adopted in
1920 for the civil service, and, as Allen (1960: 84) notes, this worked

reasonably well while prices and incomes were rising in the private sector. Even at this time, however, the Civil Service Clerical Association called into question the particular concept of model employer being employed, arguing that the government ought to be 'tempered by the reflection that the State cannot take its morals from below, but should set standards of itself from above which should be an example for the private employer to follow' (in ibid.: 85). This debate emerged in full in the debate around the Royal Commission [Tomlin] on the civil service between 1929 and 1931 (shades of which can also be seen in evidence to the Local Government Pay Commission of 2003 – see LGPC 2003). The Treasury counter-posed the staff side's view of model employment with the argument that wages 'should not be unduly high' as this would make the civil service 'a privileged class' and do an 'injustice to the community' (Allen, 1960: 86). At this point, the Tomlin Commission was led to reject the proposal that the government should be a model employer 'because it considered the phrase was meaningless' (ibid.). It went on to recommend the use of longer-run relativity in wage levels and in the economic condition of the country – a position which became known as the Tomlin Formula and was used until the 1950s to justify official negotiators' attitudes to wage claims. However, in practice, the official negotiators were 'not successful in applying the formula', with the unions consistently claiming 'that the wages of their members lagged behind those in outside industry and in the main their claims were justified' (Allen 1960: 86–7).

For local government, there was an even longer struggle for 'Whitleyism': in the end, only the Second World War made a difference. A constitution for a Whitley Council had been agreed in 1920, but when the first set of national salary scales was sent to the individual local authorities for implementation, they refused to apply the scales, repudiated the agreement, and quit the Whitley Council. Similarly, in local authority hospitals, 'no inclusive negotiation machinery had been established' prior to the Second World War: war again making the difference (Clegg & Chester, 1957: 3–5).

Thus, fundamental disagreements on the notions of model employer, comparability, and fairness were visible in this period, while material outcomes remained poor. This was to provide the real model for the government's role with its direct employees – one in which rhetoric strongly contrasted with reality, and in which even the rhetoric was confused and disputed. This term was still deeply disputed by the Second World War.

The Second World War: a new consensus?

The Second World War gave rise to more changes in the industrial relations environment:

> The indifference with which the Government had viewed the labour scene when employers were powerful was replaced by a deep consideration for industrial relations ... As in the First World War, legislation was introduced to prohibit strikes and enforce arbitration. The Government's consideration for Labour continued after the war. It wanted unions to be moderate in their demands and conciliatory in their approach to industrial differences in order to assist in the solution of national economic problems created by inflation and an adverse balance of foreign trade. (Allen 1960: 64)

The same economic problems remained to be solved when the Conservative party took office in 1951; initially the cooperation of the trade unions was also sought. However, after 1956, government was prepared to be tougher with trade unions (Allen 1960: 64–5). By this time, government was the 'nation's largest employer', and now 'attempted to enforce a policy of wage restraint on its own employees' (ibid.: 67).

A more detailed evaluation of government as direct employer in the post-Second World War era suggests the problems established for the model employer thesis in the preceding era are equally valid. For the civil service, as noted, issues of government as model employer, and of fairness and comparability, had not been resolved and material pay outcomes remained poor before the Second World War. A Royal Commission examined the principles of wage determination again in 1953–1955, after the government had exhorted workers to exercise wage restraint. The Commission 'substantially rejected the Tomlin Formula', arguing that 'fairness' should replace the notion of longer-term stability. However, as Allen (1960) notes, 'fairness ... had no precise meaning. Its definition varied with every interest group in civil service affairs' (ibid.: 87). In practice, the government had to succeed with its own employee wages policy as 'otherwise the purpose of the Government's economic policy would have been defeated, for the public sector was large and the effects of its treatment pervaded the whole economy' (ibid.: 88).

Wage restraint was therefore paramount in the government's dealings with its employees, as quickly became apparent in its broader dealings with the enlarged public sector. Nationalization after the Second World War added 2.5 million non-civil service government workers. Most were already strongly organized, following the boom in union membership prior to the war and unions' increased power during the war. Most unions were also affiliated to the TUC and Labour party and able to take political action. In these circumstances the practices of free collective bargaining continued, not because of any great commitment by the government to a model employer role but because of pragmatic considerations. Nationalized workers had high expectations of the new system, but the results with respect to earnings and conditions of work in the post-Second World War decade were disappointing and problems arose for a wide variety of pay settlements (Allen 1960: 91–108).

To the extent that the government had ever accepted a role as model employer, this position was now clearly and explicitly at an end, and 'the Government's anomalous position as a large-scale employer, conciliator, and regulator-in-chief of the economy' (ibid.: 113) was laid bare:

> The Government gave priority to its role as regulator of the economy. Where this, in the Government's opinion, required a policy of wage restraint, the Government applied the policy directly to its own employees. It did so not only because it was the easiest course to take but also because it acted as an example to private industry...it applied its policy to the sections of its labour force which had the least ability to harm the economy through strike action. (ibid.: 113)

Overt incomes policies, applied with particular force to public sector workers, were to follow in the next two decades (see Winchester 1983: 164–76), and were to further erode the concepts of model employer and comparability.

Taken as a whole, the historical evidence we have presented makes the case for much more sophisticated approaches to the model employer concept as applied to states: usages of this concept, along with associated terminologies such as 'fairness' or 'comparability', varied in nuance with the interest group employing it and the circumstances of the time. The approach also develops a more dynamic understanding of state interactions with their own employees: national bargaining was *achieved* rather than granted and the outcomes from it were equally time and pressure dependent.

Myths and material realities: modern state employment

A further part of the case for sensitive analysis lies in the material, and structural, realities of modern public sector employment. The state sector internationally is now not only a major area of employment, but also a major area of employment for women. Class and race also provide important schisms within, and sources of disadvantage for, public sector employment and pay; but owing to constraints of space, we will focus on gender.[11] The feminized nature of public services is much neglected in most accounts, past and present, but has major implications for analyses centred on the state as model employer. More than five and a half million workers are directly employed in the UK state sector (*Labour Market Trends* 2006: 1) – just over a fifth of all those employed in the national economy. At the level of the gendered composition of employment in the UK economy as a whole, around a third of all women who are employed work in the public sector, while within the public sector itself women are by far the largest group. In fact, there has been increasing 'feminization' of the public sector in the United Kingdom over time. Estimates do vary, not least because of definitional problems arising around the scope and boundaries of the public sector itself; but from a position of just under half the workforce in 1971 (Beaumont 1992: 34–5), women now account for *up to four fifths* of total public sector employment.[12] This compares with an employment rate for women of under half (around 46 per cent) in the economy as a whole. The treatment of women in the state sector is therefore a major concrete 'test' for the exploration of government as model employer.

And here the facts are sobering. Firstly, if the public sector at large is an example of gender segregation, the patterns of horizontal and vertical segregation within individual service sectors, and even within discrete 'occupations', are striking and embedded. The two largest individual sectors are health and local government, jointly accounting for some 78 per cent of all public sector employment, with 1.4

Table 5.1   NHS hospital and community health services: total employed staff by sex

Staff Group	Males (%)	Females (%)
Total employed staff	21	79
Medical and dental staff	64	36
Senior managers and managers	42	58
Qualified nursing, midwifery, and health visiting staff	11	89
Qualified ambulance staff	72	28
Support to doctors and nursing staff*	12	88

* Includes nursing auxiliaries and assistants, health care assistants, and clinical support workers amongst others.
Source: Adapted from DoH (2005) in Thornley (2006: 347).

and 2.8 million workers respectively (*Labour Market Trends* 2004: 273). Both are highly feminized: women account for four fifths of workers in health and almost three-quarters in local government (figures for England and Wales, LGPC 2003: 10–16). Within health, as can be seen in Table 5.1, women are proportionately underrepresented – relative to the number of women employed overall – at the *top* of the hierarchy *and overrepresented in the lower echelons*. And, as can be seen, horizontal segregation is also apparent, with women, for example, far more likely to be employed as nurses than as ambulance workers. If we consider occupations, nursing, for instance, there is again evidence of vertical and horizontal segregation (Thornley 2001: 97). Similarly, local government as a whole – encompassing occupations like teaching, social work, council staff – also exhibits vertical and horizontal segregation. This can be seen at its most striking in the largest bargaining group, Local Government NJC services, where 1.6 million workers are employed and which includes staff such as home carers, social workers, and non-teaching staff in schools. It can be seen from Table 5.2 that horizontal segregation can here be extreme (compare refuse collectors with school cooks, for example).

Disproportionately high numbers of part-time workers also characterizes both these sectors. While part-time work accounts for around a quarter of overall UK employment, it accounts for two fifths of employment in health, and almost half in local government, rising to 55 per cent for the 1.6 million workers in NJC services. The proportion of women working part-time is, however, even higher – 47

Table 5.2 Local government NJC services employment: total employed staff
by sex (select occupations)

Staff group (occupation)	Males (%)	Females (%)
Total employed staff	25	75
Chief officers/senior managers	65	35
Planning officers	71	29
Accountants	56	44
School caretakers	84	16
Refuse collectors	89	11
School cooks	7	93
Home care workers	3	97

Source: Thornley (2006: 347).

and 67 per cent of women in these sectors respectively work part-time (Thornley 2006: 348). Here the incidence of gendered part-time work is even more extreme than in the economy as a whole.[13] Such part-time work is also concentrated in the female-dominated occupations, and is relatively rare in the male-dominated occupations.

The segregation and high levels of part-time work evidenced above are also reflected in unequal and low pay in the public sector. So far as full-time workers are concerned there is still a sizeable gender pay gap in the public sector, and contrary to the perhaps overly sanguine views of much recent commentary on the UK 'model employer' state this has been relatively *sticky* in recent years. Currently, the 'internal' gender pay gap between women and men full-time workers within the public sector stands at about 18 per cent, while the 'external' full-time gender pay gap between women in the public sector and men in the private sector stands at around 19 per cent. There has been only a marginal shift in these figures over the period of New Labour.[14] While this gap appears superficially better than the private sector gender pay gap, it is the case that the public sector generally employs a relatively high proportion of women in 'professional' and 'non-manual' occupations – a feature of public services employment consistently overlooked – and has a generally higher qualification level than for the whole economy. Moreover, women in the public services have a typically mature age profile, and an above economy average length of service (see Thornley 2006: 349).

In any event, the real extent of the gender pay gap in the public sector can hardly be properly captured by considering comparisons based *only* on full-time workers, not least given the disproportionately higher numbers of part-time women workers employed. Part-time women workers typically have a much larger pro rata pay gap with male full-time workers – in the public sector as in the private sector – and this influence on the aggregate gender pay gap, when properly understood as pertaining to both full-time *and* part-time women workers, can be extreme where high numbers of part-time women workers are employed.

Moreover, the aggregate nature of these kinds of comparison conceals the real variation in gendered pay outcomes in different parts of the public sector and for different occupations. For example, a disaggregated independent study of local government workers (see Thornley 2003a) found that their gross pay deteriorated from 1992 to 2002 when measured against either the economy-wide average or the private sector; and reflecting disadvantages of class and gender NJC workers, manual workers and women workers all fared particularly badly.[15] In the health services too, closer study has shown that more than half of all nurses, an overwhelmingly female occupation and the single largest occupation in health, have basic salary levels well below the economy-wide median, and most are clustered at the lower end of the pay grades, with long periods of deterioration.[16] Female registered nurses working full-time still earn less than the national average and considerably less than the national average for male workers; while nursing auxiliaries (NAs) and health care assistants (HCAs) have fared even worse over matching periods, and continue to do so (Thornley 1998, 2005).

The impact on pay outcomes of part-time work can also be extreme in particular areas. For example, the majority of part-time women in NJC local government services earned less than £11,000 basic earnings pro rata equivalent in 2002.[17] In line with this, an estimate of the 'real' gender pay gap for women in NJC services, which takes proper pro rata account of the composition of the workforce, is 35 per cent, roughly *twice* the aggregate 'internal' gender pay gap for the public sector reported above (Thornley 2003a). In health too, where part-time work is most prevalent in the lower echelons, some of the lowest-paid workers (for example, HCAs) have seen relative pay deteriorate not only against male, but also against female comparators, with a concomitantly sharp polarization in pay levels and a widening of the gender pay gap (see Thornley 1998, 2005, 2008).

The extent of low pay in the sector, and its correspondence with gendered employment, is also poorly captured by headline splashes on gender pay gaps calculated for full-time workers. More than one quarter of full-time women and up to three-quarters of full-time manual women in the public sector are low paid when measured against the Council of Europe decency threshold using gross pay (Thornley 2006: 350). Within local government overall, the average earnings of full-time female manual workers fall below this threshold. And in NJC services the majority of staff, over 80 per cent of women and 90 per cent of part-time women are low paid on this measure (using basic pay) – over two thirds of all NJC workers earned less than £14,000 basic pay in 2002 (Thornley 2003a). In health, around a third of nurses overall are low-paid, and almost all HCAs and NAs (Thornley 1998, 2005, 2008). Low pay is also prevalent in administrative, clerical, and ancillary work in both health and local government, and low-paid workers across these sectors form large pockets just above the level of the National Minimum Wage (a much lower measure than the Council of Europe measure).

Taken as a whole, the facts of segregation, unequal, and low pay in a feminized public sector sit uncomfortably with conceptualizations of the state as a 'model employer', as potentially gender biased an intellectual construct – when not being ironically deployed – as it might be possible to imagine. However, the resurgence of this term may be partly understood through an evaluation of the effects of poor material pay outcomes in a highly unionized sector with complex industrial relations frameworks. Here, as with our earlier history of the progress of model employer concepts set in a proper contextualization of power shifts in a complex and unstable pay and industrial relations environment, the term may be seen to be employed as part normative, part rational, and part legitimation. Rather than rehearsing the detailed recent histories in the two largest sectors, local government and health (see instead, for example, Thornley et al. 2000), we reflect here on the particular experiences under New Labour.

New Labour in broader context: pay restraint and equalities

If we come now to locate the discussions of previous sections of this chapter in our understanding of New Labour's practice in public sector employment, we can see both the risks of overstating the conflict-free nature of an earlier pre-Thatcher era in the public sector, and of glossing over prior structures of disadvantage and inequality. While the position of many public sector workers deteriorated under Margaret Thatcher, these Conservative governments were not the first to squeeze; nor did Mrs Thatcher invent gender inequalities or gender segregation. Moreover, we have evidenced the persistence of a very sizeable, and badly underestimated, public sector gender pay gap under New Labour; a government that inherited, like its Conservative predecessors, a gender segregated – and increasingly feminized – workforce. To make sense of points of continuity and change here requires a long perspective, one that again identifies pressures from below as much as policy initiatives from above.

The early labour market policy of New Labour under Tony Blair promised, as we have already had occasion to note, some small concessions to hard-pressed trade unions organizing in the private sector, but with a large nod to business. For public sector employment, and reflective of the 'third way' to be discussed in the next chapter, two quickly emerged themes were of 'flexibility' and 'fairness'. The same promises in the same language were also invoked for the private sector. But there are distinguishing aspects to public sector employment – the state *is* the employer – which mean that separate consideration has to be given as to how each of these terms would be defined at the point of practical reference, and whether each could be simultaneously promoted alongside the other without creating pressures for immediate redefinition. For example, parallels could be inferred between 'flexibility' and 'fairness' on the one hand, and methods of 'rational' and 'normative' control on the other – but issues of application and compatibility still arise.

If we consider policy initiatives from above, the first point to note is that New Labour could have elected to play a strong role in addressing wider inequality directly through its own employment practice, providing a positive example to the private sector as a (normative) 'model employer'. In practice, it has broadly maintained the approach to liberalization of public services associated with previous Conservative governments, lobbied for by external interests, and has referred frequently to the need for 'prudence' in the public sector and the constraints of competing under 'globalization'. It continued Conservative party cash limits on public sector spending in its first term – the PFI being a separate development – creating considerable pressure from public service trade unions over wages. However, there have also been changes: some legislative 'favours' have been granted to individual workers and trade unions more generally in the form of new employment rights; and of particular significance for the highly feminized and unequal public sector new equalities legislation (and associated policies and policy rhetoric) have also been introduced, albeit much influenced by EU Directives.[18]

The second point to note, before considering issues of application and compatibility, is that these initiatives from above cannot be separated from pressures from below. The public sector remains relatively highly unionized; the formation by merger of UNISON in 1993, now the largest public sector union – one of the UK's largest – and one with a majority female membership (see Thornley 2006: 352–4), changed worker representation and shifted the balance of power in significant parts of the public sector. Equality, the heart of its founding constitution, has been vigorously pursued through campaigns over both low and (un)equal pay, by negotiation and litigation, and also by attempts to influence the direction of legislation (ibid.). The public sector was (and is) susceptible to litigation (see, in particular, Kingsmill 2001: 7), and Local Government Pay Commission (2003: 93–4)). Several ground-breaking cases were brought by UNISON from its formation involving millions of pounds of back pay (Thornley 2006: 353–4); since then a number of 'no win, no fees' lawyers have increased the number of cases sharply – with significant implications (see Thornley 2007a). This litigious background has provided pressure for new payment systems across the public sector,[19] with equalities necessarily included in the government's modernization agenda (ibid.) and more recent equalities legislation including an explicit focus on the public sector.[20]

The policies of New Labour have, in practice, exhibited a readily identified internal tension between the stated objectives of 'fairness' and 'flexibility'; and its approach to the public sector is symptomatic of wider stresses with broader implications. References to the government as a model employer jostle for position in official policy documents with measures designed to cheapen labour,[21] often expressed in the guise of 'flexibility' enhancements; while de facto exhortations to lower-level employers in the public sector (for example, in hospital trusts, or in town councils) to 'sort out' the situation sit uneasily with the lack of central government resourcing for what would be an extremely costly exercise (Thornley 2006: 354–5).[22] These stresses have been felt through attacks on pensions, a bitter struggle over pay decentralization, contracting out and privatization, and over the 'two-tier workforce' and labour substitution (ibid.). They have also been felt, as might be predicable from historical experience, through industrial action (ibid. – see also Coates 2005c: 92–3; Thornley 2007a).

Summing up

If the state sector is a very important one, and not least from the viewpoint of the workers who are employed within, there is also an evolved propensity for governments to declare that the role of the state in employment is that of a model employer – and not only in the particular case of Britain, our principal focus in this chapter. Faced with this claim, an historically informed circumspection is demanded if progress is to be made in picking apart its many strands; because references to the model employer state have appeared time and again, but in many guises – as irony, reprimand, or encouragement, as a declared political aspiration, as a union appeal to the public or bargaining chip with employers, as well as the state's own self-declared status. Latterly, and by contrast with a substantially more nuanced literature developing around the topic of the model employer business firm, the model employer state is in danger of becoming the positive description of choice for British academic commentary on public sector employment. In this chapter, we draw upon earlier academic traditions – as well as contemporary US perspectives on model employer rhetoric in the business sector – to suggest a way of understanding the stresses and continuities evident in the state sector. The elusive concept of the model employer – its polemical aspects and elisions – becomes more explicable if grounded in a careful assessment of the contexts in which it appears. There are complex 'normative' and 'rational' connotations – as we adopt these terms – sensitive in framing and in execution to trade unions and pressures from below, but also reflecting in form the rhetoric and asymmetries of each succeeding era. The seeming paradox between two poles of rhetoric emanating from the same government quarters regarding the centrality of the state's social role as a model employer on the one hand, and the need for efficiencies and flexibilities to be reaped from liberalization and deregulation on the other – including outsourcing and privatization of employment, and under the pressure of international agencies and agreements on services provision – may prove to be reconcilable if we commence these kinds of consideration. Model employer rhetoric can be an obvious legitimizing prop for governments seeking to restrain costs at the expense of state sector employees, as much as a concessionary stance. In this connection too the potential for complex displays of self-deception on the part of states is also apparent.

We make the case accordingly for a more circumspect – and gendered – view of the state in its relations with employees, observing points of continuity as well as change. And we warn against exaggerating the impact of Thatcherism in this sphere, either by assuming a golden age of state employment practices beforehand, or a substantially improving set of state employment practices afterwards – and certainly not as a simple corollary of top-down policies conceived in the absence of pressures. The risk of either stance is illustrated when we consider (even briefly) gender relations in state employment – a structure of profound segregation and inequality of outcomes which predates Thatcherism and, one can speculate, will post-date New Labour. We draw out some of the implications for this, and building upon the windows opened up to the character of British capitalism today, in the remaining chapters of this book.

6
New Ways or the Abject State

In this chapter we come next to two parallel debates. The first, as observed in the introduction to this book, is focused on the United Kingdom and deals with the premises and consequences of the New Labour project. We broach this debate by first observing some of the difficulties attaching to any attempt to 'theorize' the New Labour project vis-à-vis some of the intellectual influences which have been claimed on its behalf, before coming to 'third way' thinking and the efforts of Anthony Giddens. We consider this orientation towards New Labour in two ways: as a particular kind of ideological reflex – legitimation as much as reflection – and on its merits. It is not our intention here to add as such to existing surveys, some of a very high standard, of the political development of the New Labour project or its achievements if judged against stated goals, although we draw on important work of this kind. Rather, we are concerned with deepening our understanding of British capitalism today, observing in this connection the sometimes direct and sometimes elliptical ways in which comparisons have been brought to bear with policy predilections in other capitalist economies. The second debate, drawing together an international set of contributors and contributions, is specifically concerned with the diverging experiences of different capitalist economies. In an obvious sense, our contribution to this second stream of debate – and building upon the studies comprising the main text of the book up to this point – sits in one part with our assessment of whether or not 'third way' thinking does stand up on merit, and with our own judgement on developments in the United Kingdom, as one experience of capitalism.

Theorizing New Labour

In many ways, it is easier to list the items said to have been decisively rejected than to identify a consistently defined set of positive precepts guiding New Labour. Thus, for example, Tony Blair's campaign in 1994 and 1995 to ditch Clause IV of the old Labour Party Constitution, probably drafted by Sidney Webb, which committed the party, at least in principal, to a socialism with an active 'common ownership'[1]. Or, to take another instance, the soon to be Chancellor of the Exchequer Gordon Brown's very public courting of 'prudence with a purpose' – '[b]y 1997 the prudent economics of Gordon Brown had the official IMF seal of approval and were received acquiescently by his party and unperturbed by the City' (Driver and Martell 1998: 32)[2] – widely interpreted as signalling the end of anything like a Keynesian view of demand management. That events of the past year have seen each of these 'abandonments' at least partially reclaimed, and in spectacular circumstances, is not, at this point, the issue. It is perhaps too blank a statement to say that New Labour emerged solely in the form of a series of renunciations, and the next section makes the necessary qualification. However, insofar as the pitch for big ideas is concerned, early attempts by Blair and others to set out a 'vision' saw various framing concepts tried on first for size, before dropping away.

For example, Amitai Etzione, and North American 'communitarianism', were names very much in vogue amongst writers in Britain seeking to attribute, or to help build, or to speculate on, the emerging character of Labour in the 1990s – as each was briefly taken up by policy circles associated with the early years of the New Labour project. But after the initial brief flurry, Etzioni – and communitarianism – rarely seem to surface as references, outside of commentaries developed in a specifically academic milieu. This is not to deny that interpretation here is far more complex than these comments alone imply and perhaps most particularly for issues of social policy. For example, Simon Prideaux identifies communitarianism with a 'focus upon family, community, social discipline and responsibility', rather than a 'blanket bestowal of rights' (Prideaux: 2005: 33) (and referencing here Bowring 1997); and certainly the kind of rhetoric one might draw from this has proved an abiding feature of New Labour policy presentation. Issues arise, however, as to how one treats any coupling of 'rights and responsibilities', since similar resonances exist in long standing traditions within Britain's own political discourse – and with no particular claim to an ownership stake from the centre or left.[3] In much the same way, while Tony Blair's much publicized claims to private intellectual adventures with figures like John Macmurray, a Scottish philosopher, are certainly not without interest, what exactly to make of this kind of profession – the declaration broke to a Scottish newspaper – remains hard to decide (see Prideaux 2005: chapter 4).

A rather easier, or at least, less difficult, judgement is possible on perhaps the most concretely envisaged formulations of an alternative approach towards what might still be recognized as a form of social democracy, when in the middle part of the 1990s much talk turned on the idea of a 'stakeholder economy'. At its most general level stakeholding invites notions of 'incorporation' and 'inclusion' within a potentially pluralist vision, and more so in less conservative formulations which recognize at the point of construction that capitalism left to its own devices can exist quite easily alongside social and economic exclusion for masses of people.[4] Driver and Martell (1998: 51–60) provide a good sense of the terms of this debate, commencing with a 1996 speech delivered by Tony Blair as recently elected leader of the opposition, calling for a 'stakeholder economy, in which opportunity is available to all, advancement is through merit and from which no group or class is set apart or excluded' (ibid.: 51–2, citing Blair 1996). This spurred a lively to-and-fro in opinion-forming circles, contributions on the specifically economic front diverging sharply on details and bifurcating into those entailing more interventionist reforms to be enacted by the state, and those entailing less. Will Hutton's (1995) *The State We're In*, a bestselling book that appeared just before Blair's public float for stakeholding, is selected by Driver and Martell (ibid.: 53) as a 'radical' example, with proposals including compulsory obligations on firms concerning the representation and constitutional incorporation of employee interests, and wide-ranging reforms of corporate governance on issues like company information and accounting practices.

One noteworthy feature of the stakeholder debate is the appearance within of examples drawn from different experiences of capitalism, not least in Germany and Japan. But even while critical discussion commenced on the aptness or otherwise of the stakeholder metaphor and on its merits and demerits as a basis for policy formulation, and even as sides were being drawn up on the relevance of 'foreign' models of capitalism, Tony Blair's enthusiasm waned. Driver and Martell (1998) observe that while the 'early days of New Labour' saw European capitalism, 'more particularly German (or Rheinland) model capitalism' cited as an 'attractive model', this 'faded from New Labour thinking between 1995 and 1997' (ibid.: 46, 49–50). In the same way, in an overlapping and only slightly distended timeframe, the New Labour stakeholding debate died away. As with other early 'pitches' for ideas, less and less was heard about 'stakeholding' models from figures associated with New Labour, following Blair's 1997 election victory.

Perhaps not surprisingly, the increasingly dominant 'theorization' of New Labour proved to be the far more elusive and eliding concept of the 'third way', a much deployed term with a chequered political past regarding left and right. In this instance, if an intellectual heritage can be claimed here, vis-à-vis New Labour, this has tended to go to the sociologist Anthony Giddens – 'allegedly Tony Blair's favourite intellectual', according to the jacket-cover blurb for Giddens (1998) supplied by Will Hutton – who acknowledges in turn intellectual and policy predecessors (see Giddens ibid: vii–iii, 25–6; also Giddens 2000:1–7). In these formative works, Giddens commences from a particular reading of the past – the 'final discrediting of Marxism', the 'dissolution of the "welfare consensus"', the 'very profound social, economic and technological changes that helped bring these about' – with globalization, depoliticization, and individualism all invoked in ways that imply largely inexorable impressions on the world stage. The case is made accordingly for 'social democrats' to 'revise their pre-existing views more thoroughly than most have done so far', in order to 'find a third way' (Giddens 1998: vii).

Warning that this label 'is of no particular significance in and of itself', the key selling point in Giddens (1998) is that the reader should understand his own specific usage and formulation of 'social democratic renewal' as a general process, all the better to understand the 'new' in New Labour (see ibid.: vii–viii).[5] Thus, for example, the view that New Labour was essentially influenced by the United States rather than Europe – a popular stance also consistent with one understanding of the demise of the stakeholder debate – is rejected. Rather, for Giddens 'virtually all Continental social democratic parties' had already made a similar break with the past as New Labour was now making. The need was to catch up with the most advanced of them in order to be a 'sparking point for creative interaction between the US and Continental Europe' (ibid.: viii–ix), employing valuable lessons learned from the unique experiences of Thatcherism. Set in this context, Giddens' third way thereby invoked from the outset an appreciation that –

> the economic theory of socialism was always inadequate, underestimating the capacity of capitalism to innovate, adapt and generate increasing productivity. Socialism also failed to grasp the significance of markets as informational devices, providing essential data for buyers and sellers. These inadequacies only became fully revealed with intensifying processes of globalization and technological change from the early 1970s onwards. (ibid.: 5)

while making the case for modernization for a modern world, 'to transcend both old-style social democracy and neoliberalism' (ibid.: 25–6); a perspective maintained more or less consistently through a growing list of restatements in response to criticism.[6]

Anxious to allay fears that what this entails might be nothing more than 'warmed up neoliberalism' (see Giddens 1998: 25) – the concessions to Thatcherism in the passage quoted above, and a point to which we return, could hardly be starker – there is an extensive discussion of more progressively attuned themes, although while the mood music is rich the translation of the libretto is less certain. Nonetheless, it is important, for example, to weave alliances from the 'threads of lifestyle diversity' (ibid.: 45); and show due respect to our 'relationship to nature' (ibid.: 64); and provide a 'new relationship between individual and community', 'a redefinition of rights and obligations' (ibid.: 65); while maintaining the 'democratized family' (ibid.: 93). There must also be a 'more cosmopolitan version' of nationhood and democracy (see ibid.: 129–41).

At the same time, however, and with perhaps clearer practical policy implications, to the extent that inequality is an issue, it should be addressed through a 'redistribution of possibilities' (understood as inclusion and community building) rather than 'after the event redistribution' – of realized income and wealth – as 'the traditional working class has largely disappeared' (Giddens 1998: 100–4). The logic of the connections being established here is not difficult to challenge. However, our point at this stage is that Giddens has very little to say – for example – about earnings inequalities. Moreover, gender inequalities seem pretty much a non-issue: with less than a handful of references to women in an essay of some one hundred and fifty pages, it is simply contended that gender-based inequalities are diminishing, and therefore one imagines not a substantive problem to be further explored with regards to the 'third way'. In a later work, 'the growing equality between women and men, a trend that is also worldwide, even if it still has a long way to go' is cited as one of Giddens' major examples of 'spectacular' 'global transformations' (Giddens and Hutton 2001a: 2, 27; 2001b: 216) – but one so interesting, apparently, and so self-evident, that no further policy attention is warranted.

As a body of commentary, the third way strand of thought is interesting because it is both an attempt to explain New Labour (this is made explicit by Giddens) and to further influence it. It seeks to provide, whatever one might make of it, a degree of 'intellectual legitimacy', and a claim to policy coherence that might otherwise be absent. Elements of each can also be found in the communitarian and stakeholding debates: but if these also indicate the search for a big idea, the Giddens thesis is of particular interest from the viewpoint of the themes of this chapter, concerning legitimation and denial.

If we commence with the question of legitimation – and put to one side the markedly degendered features of the third way as an intellectual construct – then it is impossible not to be struck by how far Giddens goes in conceding to Thatcherism. It is true, and the qualification is a necessary one, that the stance is adopted that a revivified centre left might flourish because of the space afforded by the difficulties experienced by 'neoliberalism', 'in trouble' because of tension between 'its two halves – market fundamentalism and conservatism' (Giddens 1998: 15). But if we refer again to the passage cited above on what went wrong with capitalism in the 1970s, what leaps out is the weight given to the inadequacies of the economic theory of *socialism*. There is reference to international forces – 'intensifying processes of globalization' – and a hint perhaps of something like, or akin to, a post-Fordist transitionary argument, in the oblique aside on 'technological change from the early 1970s'.[7] But we can also wonder if at some level Giddens also shares Mrs Thatcher's view that the crisis of capitalism in this period was caused *by* socialism – and hence a crisis *for* socialism.

In reconsidering the 'third way' as the distillation of an intellectual surrender, however, we cannot go too far, and credit must be given to the dissonance of some of its elements. For example, Giddens' early explanation and defence of New Labour as simply the outcome of a late process of modernization already undergone by 'virtually all' Continental parties of the left is hard to reconcile with Tony Blair's prompt 'torpedoing' of a EU employment plan proposed by the French socialist party leader Lionel Jospin in 1997, or his subsequent alliances forged five years later with the likes of Silvio Berlusconi, and in opposition to continental left (and right) parties, to push the case for enhanced flexibilities and softer employment regulation in the EU, and further marketization of public sector services (see Coates 2005c: 85, 229).[8] If this suggests some oversimplification in Giddens' historical assessment of revisionist politics on the European mainland, the gap between his own conception and New Labour practice also confirms – even if in a backhanded way – his independence of thought. Equally, the concessionary tone to the insights of Mrs Thatcher, regarding the failings of 'old style social democracy' is marked, and far from subtle, on economic matters.

We have already warned against any simple conflation of state ownership within capitalism, or state regulation of capitalism, with socialism. And the role of nationalization, and of promised reregulation, as well as a putative rediscovery of Keynesianism, in the face of the latest economic and financial crisis for capitalism, indicates perhaps that whatever Giddens' personal achievements, he is no historian. However, before coming to this crisis, in the next chapter, a rounded assessment demands some sense of the real economic (and social) achievements of New Labour in office.

The successes and failures of New Labour

Here we could do no better than to begin with David Coates' comprehensive review of the policy objectives to which New Labour committed itself over its first two terms in office.[9] Coates (2005c), the most detailed and rigorous analysis to date to carefully distinguish the extent to which New Labour has met objectives it has set

for itself, from a broader intellectual assessment, offers a methodo-
logically distinctive approach that assesses the practical successes
and failures of New Labour in terms both of its own selected objectives as well as more broadly.

In each respect, a striking characteristic of New Labour early on
was the relatively proscribed list of objectives actually set. In fact, for
Coates what emerges as new about New Labour was the 'limited range
of policy instruments' originally envisaged, and a 'refusal to deploy'
standard policy instruments that could be associated with the party
as it was before – that is with 'Old Labour' – and particularly where
these could be construed as a barrier to entrepreneurship. Thus the
repudiation of public ownership, of state control or direction of private industry, of plans for a state investment bank, of the extension
of industrial democracy, and so forth. Instead, the objectives were to
strengthen growth and productivity through competitiveness based
on higher quality, skill, innovation, and reliability (Coates 2005c:
31–3). The state was thus to act as a lubricant in the economy, working in partnership with industry, embracing free trade, controlling
inflation, containing taxation and public spending; and with key
objectives including attracting inwards foreign direct investment,
strengthening research and development, and maintaining flexible
labour markets and enhancing the movement from welfare to work –
as well as the new national minimum wage (ibid.: 34–5). Investment
in people was seen as paramount and as the key both to economic
success and social justice, with the aim of achieving 'economic dynamism' alongside 'social cohesion': 'each could only be enhanced by
policies which recognized that "the role of government has changed:
today it is to give people the education, skills, technical know-how to
let their own enterprise and talent flourish in the new market place" '
(ibid.: 36).[10]

It is this position (principally) which constitutes the necessary
qualification to the opening remark in the last section observing
that New Labour was unveiled to the public largely through a series of renunciations of earlier policy positions. Moreover, and the
point requires emphasis, the emerging agenda envisaged benefits
in the form of social inclusion and personal advancement as well
as 'economic dynamism' as things to be jointly achieved by means
of 'education', 'skills', and 'technical know-how'.[11] At the same
time, however, we can note the change in framing also implied for

assessments of the sources of disadvantage, moving away from the 'system' to the 'personal'.

In addition, we can observe that any appraisal of the successes of New Labour on its own terms involves considering a relatively narrow set of ambitions, while developing a broader judgement on its performance also entails asking if these ambitions were enough. Insofar as this bigger question is concerned, Coates' summary assessment, judiciously balanced, is then worth considering carefully. An immediate point to note is that this 'audit' of New Labour is based on a survey (see Coates 2005c: 161–84), with a wealth of supporting references and statistics, for the period 1997 to 2004. Insofar as economic matters are concerned, the period in question thus ends before the onset of the traumas of the great international banking and credit crisis currently unfolding, although as we shall see below Coates's assessment constitutes an early warning of things to come.

Coates notes firstly some apparent positives in that the eight years from the appointment of the first New Labour government saw generally good growth rates and low inflation – that is to say, over the period 1997–2004 – and some success on unemployment figures, albeit contentious as regards to its 'true' extent and geographical spread.[12] The period saw a general rise in living standards, with some tax and policy initiative benefits for the poor, alongside the National Minimum Wage, implemented despite being the policy inheritance from a previous dispensation within the party – albeit at a 'miserably modest' level (Coates 2005c: 169). Coates also observes that a case could be made for some reduction in child poverty – child poverty thus designated having risen from about one child in ten in 1979, when Mrs Thatcher was first elected, to around one child in three by the time Tony Blair took office; and the fact that a commitment *was* firmly made (eventually) by a New Labour government 'to the halving of child poverty in one decade' and 'to its removal in two' (ibid.: 59) should not be overlooked in identifying which features of New Labour distinguish it from its Conservative predecessors.[13]

However, a wider assessment of the underlying economy and inequalities is less positive. As with Wynne Godley's early and now notably prescient concerns about private consumption debt in the United Kingdom, and Martin Weale's with housing debt, Coates infers from the existence of 'unprecedented levels of personal debt' the fact of a 'fragile underpinning of much of the UK's surface appearance of prosperity in Gordon Brown's economy ... as New Labour's Britain increasingly lived on tick' (ibid.: 170).

In fact, in addition to record levels of internal indebtedness for households and consumers, the attendant post-1997 consumer boom did 'one other thing as well':

> It fuelled a record level of international debt, by sucking in imports of manufactured goods at a much faster rate than a shrinking UK manufacture sector could pay for them with equivalent export orders. New Labour ... like the Conservatives before it, presided over a consumer sector that continued to grow rapidly and a manufacturing base that did not. (Coates 2005c: 172)

It is germane to note that because much of the impact of this debt-fuelled consumer binge was translated into jobs generation in other countries via imports, net job creation in the United Kingdom – especially since 2000 – in fact relied very heavily on the direct employment effects from increased levels of public sector spending.[14] We have already described, in a previous chapter, the political as well as economic significance of a struggling UK-based manufacturing sector in the 1970s, and its more dramatic collapse under the weight of monetarism in the 1980s. In this context, we also described and discussed the 'Singh' criterion for manufacturing competitiveness, of importance from the viewpoint of growth stability for the UK's open economy. For Coates, the continuing weakness of manufacture is one more reason for doubting the 'surface' appearances of success over the first eight years of New Labour in office (see, in particular, Coates 2005c: 161–84), with the sharply rising trade deficits reflecting the diminished size of the UK manufacturing base as well as currency issues (ibid.: 172–3; and, for example, Wilkinson 2007: 811; Coutts et al. 2007: 858) – and also, in Coates' view, two other failures under the New Labour watch: a lack of adequate business investment, and an inability to match successes in attracting overseas businesses to Britain with an upgraded performance for operations already sourced in the United Kingdom (Coates 2000c: 173–4).[15] It is hard to disagree with Coates' summary view that New Labour failed to generate the 'supply side revolution' promised in its policy prospectus (ibid.: 178). For example, Coutts et al. (ibid.: 847) argue that manufacturing output did not grow at all under New Labour.[16]

(We have previously made largely consistent observations on trends in the manufacture of automotive products in the United Kingdom, a policy 'flagship' sector.)

At the same time, and despite some policy attention to the 'poor' noted above, Coates notes that the wider picture on inequalities has been poor:

> Rising social wealth was no more equally distributed in UK society by New Labour policies than it had been by Conservative ones. Inequality remains a real feature of New Labour Britain ... [which] remained towards the bottom of the European Poverty League. (Coates, 2005c: 169–70)

And we might add to this. Overall income and earnings inequalities continued to widen for most of the period of New Labour's watch (see, for instance, on both points, Thornley 2003: 93–5; Griffiths and Wall 2007: 261–2, 267), and a recent poverty study finds that: 'the intensity of the experience of poverty ... worsened for those who [had] become or remained poor' (Angeriz and Chakravarty 2007: 1000–1). Moreover, the overall poverty rate of working age adults has remained broadly constant, while the rate for those in working households has risen (Palmer et al. 2006 cited in Theodore 2007: 936–7).[17] Gender inequality remains significant and the gender pay gap has not markedly reduced: we have already noted this for public sector workers, but the same point is also true economy wide. For example, a detailed investigation for the period 1997–2001 showed a polarization of earnings within the female workforce, and only very modest improvement in the gender pay gap – 'simply in line with previous trends' (Thornley 2003: 94), and with women's part-time earnings generally remaining particularly poor by EU standards (ibid.: 95). Looking back from the vantage point of the latest year for which statistics are available (2007), we can observe in fact that the New Labour period in office has seen several individual years in which the gender pay gap widened – including in 2007 itself. Our calculation of the current annual mean pay gap between women and men as a whole stands at 28 per cent for full-time workers, and 38 to 40 per cent for part-time workers, pro-rata.[18] On current trends, and despite the 'spectacular' and 'global' transformations claimed by Giddens, estimated 'equalization' dates for the United Kingdom vary between 2085 and 2195.[19]

The 'true character' of New Labour Britain identified by Coates is thus one in which the bigger ambitions of the Blair and Brown governments remained unfulfilled. UK-based manufacturing is dependent on low wages and long hours, features of employment recognisably characteristic of the British economy as a whole, so that Britain's face is firmly set against the 'more progressive elements of EU labour codes': 'wage rates remain low (and unequal) by Western European standards, the length of the UK working week remains long, levels of stress in UK offices and factories remain high, and UK skill levels, by contrast, remain inadequate' (Coates 2005c: 179). At the same time, with little progress being made in narrowing the gap with Europe either in terms of the experience of work, or of levels of skill and education attained, or of equality, aspirations to match the US economy have floundered (ibid.: 84), for all the homage paid. For Coates, this leaves the United Kingdom somewhere between America and Europe, and poor on both counts.

This last conclusion is worth noting, since it is perhaps too often overlooked just how different the economy of the United Kingdom is from that of the United States, not only in terms of its size but also in terms of its compositional structure, productivities, and trajectories. For example, the experience of manufacturing in the United States during the Clinton years was quite different from that of the United Kingdom, playing a far more defining role for growth.[20] In sum, the record on economic and equality outcomes does not support any internal claim on the part of New Labour, over its first eight years in office, to have achieved 'economic efficiency' with 'social justice'; while, more generally, Coates' survey flags up a series of underlying problems with economic and distributional fundamentals. In this, and even before coming to events now unfolding, the limits of the 'third way' are evident.

Theorizing varieties of capitalism: third ways and abject states

At this juncture, and while deferring some final comments until the closing part of this book, it is appropriate to ask how this sits with regard to the broader models or varieties of capitalism debate, concerned with the study, as Coates (2005b: x) puts it, of 'capitalism versus capitalism', and where we locate against it our earlier chapters. Let us first observe that for Coates, and in the context of a methodological discussion to which we will certainly return, 'capital–labour tensions' within 'capitalist models' must be central to any serious analysis, a prognosis with which we would entirely agree. At the same time, attention must be given to how 'interaction between capitalist models', as well as their 'shared experience of common global trends' can act so as to '[corrode] the viability of … internal settlements between classes', thus undermining the always contingent conditions upon which the viability of any model rests (ibid.: 121–4). In this regard, and here again we agree entirely, Coates has consistently emphasized the dangers of too strong an attachment to any particular national capitalist model when analysis is concerned with identifying the sources of the changes observed over time in its articulation, and given the crises to which capitalism *sui generis* is prone.

Let us recall in this regard the weight we give in the opening stages of this book to several recent contributions – Glyn (2006) and Klein (2007) – each of which in its own way emphasizes the fact that the 1980s saw a sharp movement within what is generally portrayed as the Anglo-American axis of capitalism against the grain of social and economic development in the decades following the Second World War. But we also noted and subsequently expanded upon an important distinction. For Glyn, there is perhaps something of an inevitability of the movement against organized labour and existing 'internal settlements' in the 1970s, as the 'golden age' ended – and not only in the United Kingdom and United States, but as a consequence of a 'crisis of capitalism' engendered more universally by trade unions on the one hand, and international competition on the other. We have suggested that there is a great deal of contrary evidence extant on this claim. By contrast, for Naomi Klein far more space is allowed the politically opportunistic features of what is nowadays summed up under Thatcherism for studies of the United Kingdom. In this regard, we have suggested an alternative way of understanding the earlier crisis of Britain's industrial capitalism in a way which accords with this sensibility, rejecting inter alia a 'profit squeeze' hypothesis for the 1970s and a linear reading of developments thereafter. At the same time, and on the question of 'shocks' – political as well as economic – we propose that 'intellectual' as well as 'practical' conversion must be given due weight in understanding the later phenomenon of New Labour as a post-Thatcher project.

From a methodological viewpoint, there is nothing in our suggested framing of political and economic developments in Britain
in the run-up to the first Thatcher government which does not sit
easily – subject of course to further testing – with Coates. But neither is it the case that Glyn's perspective would fall foul of a general
injunction that what is needed is a carefully weighted judgement of
the kind that Coates prescribes:

> [T]he post-war performance and contemporary difficulties of the
> various capitalist models manifest themselves at the level of fac-
> tors of production, and are given expression in particular sets of
> institutional practices; but those practices are themselves driven
> by the balance and character of class forces by which they are
> infused, while the trajectory of the economies they sustain are
> centrally informed by the position occupied by those classes in
> the wider system of global accumulation characteristic of world
> capitalism as a whole'. (2005a: 270)

This passage is equally consistent with Andrew Glyn's account of a
profit squeeze on capitalisms everywhere in the later part of the long
post-Second World War boom giving rise to an inevitable backlash
against organized labour, and with the more nuanced reading which
we are ascribing to Naomi Klein as well as to our suggested lines of
development for the economic contexts against which Thatcherism
was defined. However, in the first approach differences in the global
positioning of different national capitalisms within the world economy at the point where the long boom of the post–Second World
War era ended plays a distinctly second-order role: there was a general profit squeeze. For the second approach, the unique features of
Britain in comparison with Europe – quite different from France,
say, or Germany – and reflecting its own past history as a global
power, offers one way of accounting for *why* Thatcherism emerged as
it did in the United Kingdom. Certainly the crisis of capitalism was
widespread: but it is legitimate to ask why the political reaction in
Britain, and the assault on the position of its labour movement was
so severe. Here one possible starting point (building on the work of
Keith Cowling) is that Britain's industrial economy was particularly
afflicted by the destabilizing manoeuvres of corporate actors seeking
to further develop a regional basis of operations. In this scenario,

distinctions in national experiences and trajectories are equally important.

In this connection, the case studies employed in this book serve a twofold function, one clearly empirical, but the other also conceptual; because each is concerned in its own way with aspects of a state apparatus engaged in complex forms of denial. Denial of the reality of a UK-based manufacturing system subordinated to a failed competitiveness model, both from the viewpoint of Britain's workforce and of its economy; denial of the absurdities generated by a conflicting desire to expand public services while shrinking the organizational responsibility of the state vis-à-vis private interests; and denial of the profound subordination of gender and other forms of inequality to the state's own cost-cutting imperatives – hardly less savage than the private sector – as employer. And conversely, we see enacted in each case complex forms of legitimation. Our contribution to the varieties of capitalism debate, as well as further exploring 'empirical' realities in the contemporary model of British capitalism, is thus twofold: to deepen an appreciation of the likely significance of issues raised by Klein, and to push centre stage the study of forms of denial and legitimation as a key element in this kind of endeavour.

In this regard, the third ways perspective of Anthony Giddens takes on significances quite different perhaps from that which its author intended: as a study in denial, profoundly concessionary and manifestly reactive to Thatcherism as it evolved in the 1980s, not least in terms of its interpretation of earlier stresses in economy and society; and as a legitimizing construct vis-à-vis its attempt to posit New Labour as a necessary force for modernity, surpassing the limits of both socialism and market fundamentalism, and an explanation for a new worldview lending coherence to policy objectives.

The VoC approach and employment regimes: some comments

Given this, we now offer a few words, by no means intended to be exhaustive, on some other perspectives – quite distinct from that of Coates, or for that matter from the views of either Glyn or Klein, albeit with their own preoccupations – on what is relevant to the study of different varieties or models of capitalism, and their explication. In this context, we consider in more depth two particular, and influential, models or prescriptive contributions to the varieties of capitalism debate, each of interest for different reasons. The first is the Hall-Soskice model, which sets out a particular framework by which to understand the interactions between firms and states within different kinds of capitalism. The second is a critical disagreement and reformulation by Duncan Gallie, looking at employment systems. We comment briefly.

The Hall-Soskice VoC framework

To the extent that some literatures stand out more than others as representative of their time, the Hall and Soskice (2001) 'varieties of capitalism' – or VoC framework – may end up, rather like Giddens' third way, as a particular marker of a passing moment. A short and elegant critique of this model (for a list of a more extensive set of critical commentaries, and an attempted defence, see Hancké et al. [2007]) has been offered already by Colin Hay (2005), who concludes, amongst other things, that the VoC approach is insufficiently 'institutionalist' to account for observed variations amongst capitalist economies and under-resourced 'conceptually' from the viewpoint of understanding 'complex' change over time, while being guilty moreover of a peculiarly 'agentless' or 'apolitical' view of capitalism – and tending towards the 'exogenous' in explaining shocks to the system vis-à-vis capitalist economies (see ibid.: 120). Since we agree with each of these observations, while also conceding like Hay that 'it poses the right question and starts from the correct premise – the institutional variation amongst capitalist economies' (ibid.: 120), we commence with a brief précis of its main features before assessing its limitations from the viewpoint of the issues we discuss.

The Hall-Soskice (2001) framework focuses on developed market economies – treated as synonymous with capitalist economies – and is explicitly designed to answer questions concerning whether there are 'fundamental differences in national political economies conditioning economic performance and social well-being', and whether such differences can be expected to survive 'the pressures that integration into an international economy places upon nations' (ibid.: v). Private firms are taken as the crucial actors – 'the key agents of adjustment in the face of technological change or international competition whose activities aggregate into overall levels of economic performance' (ibid.: 6). Two types of political economy – ideal types – are then contrasted: liberal market economies (or LMEs), characterized by firms which coordinate activities primarily via their own internal 'hierarchies' and by means of competitive market arrangements; and coordinated market economies (or CMEs) where firms depend more heavily on non-market relations. In the first case, 'formal contracts' and 'supply and demand' rule the roost, while in the second outcomes (equilibria) are deemed to depend on strategic interaction amongst firms and 'other' actors – that is to say, 'other' than firms (ibid.: 8). These ideal types of political economy are said to operate differently in five 'spheres': industrial relations and coordination of bargaining; vocational training and education; corporate governance; interfirm relations; and employees (ibid.: 7–8) – although without discussion, for example, as to how 'industrial relations' is separated from 'employees'. A key feature of the framework is that firms will gravitate in any national economy towards the mode of coordination for which there is institutional support (ibid.: 9). It is proposed that a nation with a 'particular type of coordination' in one 'sphere' is likely to find that this is complemented by particular practices in others, so that the different types of political economy will thus differ in terms of their 'clustered' institutional practices. However, it is argued that both LMEs and CMEs are capable of providing satisfactory levels of long-run economic performance, while displaying internal differences (ibid.: 18–21). These differences are said to include the distribution of income and employment, and with LMEs typically having higher levels of income inequality (ibid.: 21).

This approach is said to entail a revision of thinking: 'the principal problem facing policy makers … is one of inducing economic actors to cooperate more effectively with each other', rather than with a strong state. In some cases, this means improving the operation of markets, in others improving equilibrium outcomes arising from strategic interaction; but in each case different policies are required by LMEs and CMEs and should be consistent. Thus the conclusion that 'deregulation is often the most effective way to improve coordination in LMEs' (ibid.: 45–50) (see also Wood 2001). Following an all too brief discussion of social policy and national interests in the international arena, the authors then focus on the challenges of globalization. These are viewed primarily as technological, accelerated by liberalization. Again the authors argue for the novelty of their approach: VoC, in contrast to 'usual' approaches which focus on issues like resistance by labour to globalization, and which anticipate convergence, predicts different dynamics in LMEs and CMEs and a 'bifurcated response' (ibid.: 54–60).

A great deal could be said (and has been said) about this arrangement of terms. That economic performance is simply an 'aggregate' of private firm activity is empirically untenable – for example, capitalist economies have a substantial state sector – and we can see immediately why the framework is criticized as 'institution-lite'. For Hall and Soskice, the micro-foundations of the model – Hay (2005: 108–11) criticizes them quite generally for favouring assumptions that provide analytical tractability at the expense of assessing key aspects of a more complex reality – flow from the 'micro' to the 'political economy as a whole', with 'systematic differences in corporate strategy across nations' paralleling 'institutional structures' within each (Hall and Soskice 2001: 14–15). Thus the United Kingdom would be a typical LME, and Germany a typical CME (ibid.: 16). This implies a static comparison between national types, with each type possessing firms of a particular hue – and with little sense that some firms organize as transnational corporations, using this position to actively leverage policy concessions from national governments.

There is no possibility, moreover, in this framework, of even beginning to frame the kind of issues discussed in this book. That destabilizing actions by internationalizing corporate entities in one period could feed into and encourage political developments with further destabilizing consequences in another – informing public perceptions of capital–labour tensions and of economic 'efficiency', and the internal course of struggles within political parties and the forms of contest between parties, all underwritten by sectoral retractions and imbalances – belongs to another conceptual universe altogether. In much the same way, it is difficult to see within the VoC framework any conceivable anticipation of the economic and financial crisis currently engulfing advanced capitalism: again, that such events could occur – and are occurring – belongs to another world. The prescribed role of the firm as the 'key agent of adjustment' is being falsified empirically, and in a way that could hardly be more dramatic, even as we take time to add this sentence: the advice to policy makers to be content with a limited sphere is not – today – apposite.

There is in fact a distinct favouring of the status quo, however it exists, in this framework: its explanatory value in explaining how this comes about is almost nugatory; that there might be any reason for deploring it, is hardly encouraged by its terms. Concerns within policy debate as these apply to Britain today – on the complexes of factors underpinning a relative failure to maintain an adequate industrial base, on the absurdities of the procedural rules governing off-balance sheet borrowing, on the social construction of gender pay gaps and other inequalities – are there only *in absentia* (unless we count the prediction that LMEs will typically have high levels of income inequality).

Employment regimes

This may be unduly harsh, and we should perhaps qualify by adding our admiration for the attempted consistency of the endeavour, once begun: but putting to one side the undetermined status of the Hall-Soskice framework – as Hay (2005:114) notes, it is not clear if it exists to organize data as a helpful heuristic device, or is intended to explain the distribution of observations as a logical-correlate – it is not hard to see in the enthusiasm with which it has been taken up by admirers the basis of a totalizing approach and, we could add, a legitimizing one, to the study of the varied experiences of capitalism.

A rather more amenable use of typology is suggested in a recent useful collection exploring employment regimes and the quality of work. Gallie (2007a, b), in introductory and concluding chapters, sets out to explore the relative merits of different theoretical frameworks in explaining differences in quality of work amongst European countries (as evidenced in the collaborative research findings reported in the book as a whole). His preferred approach involves the use of what he calls employment regimes, of which three principal types are distinguished: 'inclusive', 'dualist', and 'market'. Inclusive regimes are those where policies 'are designed to extend both employment and common employment rights as widely as possible through the population of working age'; dualist regimes are 'less concerned about overall employment levels but guarantee strong rights to a core workforce of skilled long-term employees, at the expense of poor conditions and low security of the periphery'; and market employment regimes 'emphasize minimal employment regulation and assume that market adjustments will naturally lead in the longer term to relatively high employment levels while employees' benefits will be strictly related to their marginal productivity' (Gallie 2007a: 17).[21] The role played by organized labour in policy and employment regulation is seen as critical, and the approach (laudably) encompasses issues of class and sex. Moreover, what is also laudable is the careful eschewal of any over-reaching ambitions for employment regime classifications, the use of which must be conditioned by a historically textured conscience:

> Such regime categorizations are at best very broad brush ... with important variations within countries ... regime analysis can complement, *but not substitute for*, the older traditions of 'societal' analysis which takes seriously the specificity of the historically derived institutional frameworks of particular countries. (2007: 231–2; emphasis added)

One need only add, and now with the New Labour project in mind, 'and also historically decided economic dead-ends'. But this takes us to our next chapter.

Summing up

It is not to be doubted but that there has been something qualitatively new about New Labour, and not only if the point of comparison is Old Labour. But the difficulties attending early attempts by New Labour thinkers, both within and without the party, to construct a 'big vision' framework against which to pitch, and the ultimate preference given in public discussion to Anthony Giddens' third way, points towards a void at the intellectual heart of the New Labour project: the attempt to move beyond Thatcherism while accepting, more or less uncritically, a Thatcherite understanding of economics. At the same time, and while recognizing the complexities of the issues raised, we make the case for rethinking the terms of the New Labour debate starting from a different kind of perspective, and emphasizing both the fact of, and the context to, the political as well as economic shocks of the Margaret Thatcher years with regard to the economy and society. We propose that the modern British state, in its post-Thatcher guise, has engaged in and been served by legitimating stances which have obscured, for a time, underlying problems with economic and distributional fundamentals – if New Labour emerged in a series of renunciations, it has persevered in the context of a series of abject denials.

As a closing theme in this chapter we have cautioned against too rigidly set an approach to the study of the experiences of different varieties of capitalism, taking as our example here the VoC framework associated with Hall and Soskice. We have not attempted to follow a now considerable literature in the criticism and defence of this framework, but noted rather the impossibility of framing within its terms the issues that are the subject matter not only of this chapter but also of this book as a whole. Insofar as the general methodological issues of the varieties of capitalism debate are concerned, we lean towards approaches looking for historical explanation and grounded in a sense of the tensions within capitalist economies and the interaction between capitalist economies as these inform empirically observed propensities towards crisis and change; at the same time, however, we recognize the case for a variety of perspectives.

7
The End of Things: The Great Financial Crisis

We now come to the current crisis that threatens to undermine many of the assumptions and policy predispositions of what both critics and admirers often refer to as the 'Anglo-American' model of liberal capitalism, and casts a long shadow over the global health of capitalism more generally. But even internationally, and with regards to specific questions of market regulation, the smaller partner in this unequal pairing cannot be treated as coincident with the larger, and among the questions to be addressed in this chapter is the extent to which Britain has been rendered vulnerable to the increasing scale of the world crisis as a result of its own policy failings. After a short review of salient features of the crisis, with reference both to its impact on the UK economy and the drama of its unfolding, we go on to explore the extent to which British policy mindsets and the policies pursued underlie and explain a manifest lack of preparedness for the current situation. Against this, we consider attempts to reference the crisis in the United Kingdom as a distinctly 'global' or US phenomenon. We then pose some questions regarding pragmatic and intellectual responses to the crisis. But a principal concern at this point – a prelude to the close of this book – is with unresolved weaknesses in, and political dilemmas for, the British economy on the one hand, and state denial of the portents of crisis and avoidance of responsibilities on the other.

The appearance of crisis

Financial journalists Larry Elliott and Dan Atkinson (2008) trace the first appearance of crisis back to the summer of 2007: Bear Stearns' announcement of problems with its hedge funds; Countrywide's admission of 'unprecedented disruptions' as America's biggest mortgage lender; the liquidity problems experienced by BNP Paribas as a result of its engagement with US asset-backed bonds; and early canvassing for financial assistance by Barclays Capital in London (ibid.: 14–21). In September 2007, the first run on a British bank in living memory – Northern Rock[1] – heralded to a wider public the weaknesses of financial positions within the global banking system. By early 2008, the rumbling problems with Northern Rock – 'emblematic of the state of the debt-laden UK economy' (ibid.: 72) – came to a head. Failing to find a private buyer, Chancellor Alistair Darling, successor to Gordon Brown, announced that the bank was to be nationalized. This was followed by interest rate cuts by America's Federal Reserve, and problems with the French bank Societe Generale (Elliot and Atkinson 2008: 29–32), presentiments of things rapidly to come.

In the early months of 2008, property prices and consumer confidence were falling, while borrowing conditions were being toughened and inflation rising. Western banks were seeking capital injections from sovereign wealth funds to compensate for write-downs on bad loans (ibid.: 39). From March 2008, the system went into its 'panic phase' (ibid.: 40) and the crisis hit in earnest. Lehman Brothers went bankrupt; and then Merrill Lynch, AIG, Freddie Mac, Fannie Mae, HBOS, Royal Bank of Scotland, Bradford & Bingley, Fortis, Hypo, and Alliance & Leicester all came very close to doing the same and had to be rescued (see *Observer*, 28 December 2008 for details). Western governments sunk trillions of dollars into the world banking system to prevent collapse. By the latter part of 2008, it was clear that the crisis had spread to the 'real economy': General Motors, Ford, and Chrysler pressed the US government for assistance, with similar requests being made by the auto sector in the United Kingdom. Retail trade was also being hit hard: in the United Kingdom, MFI and Woolworths, both household names, went bankrupt, with others threatening. Unemployment was rising rapidly, particularly in the United States and United Kingdom.

The impact on the UK economy at the time of writing (January 2009) has been profound. A 'technical' recession, as defined by two successive quarters of negative growth is now confirmed: the decline for the final quarter in 2008 was even higher than predicted at 1.5 per cent, the biggest fall in more than 28 years. There are openly expressed fears too about associated deflation as industrial output plummets at its fastest rate in years. As of October 2008, after eight months of successive slump, output was down by 5.2 per cent from its position a year earlier – the steepest annual decline since April 1991 – with a contraction of 4.6 per cent in the last quarter. At the same time, Britain's trade deficit in goods with the rest of the world, already negative, has widened, standing at £7.75 bn for the month of October 2008 and rising to a record £8.3 bn in November (*Guardian* 9 December 2008; also National Statistics 18 January 2009). The December 2008 *Engineering Outlook* survey predicts that manufacturing will be hit hard in 2009, with the number of people working in the sector predicted to plummet from 2.78 mn to 2.69 mn – a drop equivalent to 90,000 full-time jobs (*Personnel Today* 1 December 2008). The auto industry has been undergoing a particular crisis, not least because of the drop in consumer demand. British vehicle production dropped by 33 per cent in November 2008 compared to the previous year. Nissan is set to cut 1200 jobs at its Sunderland factory – around a quarter of its British manufacturing workforce (*Independent* 8 January 2009). Honda has announced that it will halt production at its Swindon plant for the months of April and May 2009, in addition to a two-month stoppage over February and March previously announced. Jaguar Land Rover's Indian owner, Tata, has injected money into the ailing car company to save it from immediate cash-flow problems, but 450 job cuts have now been announced and government assistance is still being sought (*Guardian* 14 January 2009). Toyota and JCB announced production cuts over Christmas (*Guardian* 5 January 2009). The situation in the United Kingdom (and Europe) is now so severe that EU ministers are seeking to coordinate their responses to bailing out the auto industry and to accelerate aid from the European Investment Bank (*Guardian* 16 January 2009).

The condition of the retail trade and service sector is also badly deteriorated. Despite a government cut in the VAT rate in December 2008, the value of retail sales has been poor, making it the worst December in over a decade, with food retail the only area not to suffer significantly. The largest UK fashion retailer, Marks and Spencer, has announced store closures and over a thousand job cuts (*BBC News* 6 January 2009); the Woolworths' closure involves 27,000 job losses; and around 100,000 job losses are expected in retail overall in 2009 (*Times* 7 January 2009). After an already sharp rise in the number of retail insolvencies in 2008, it is predicted that up to 1400 retailers will be forced out of business in 2009 (*Guardian* 1 January 2009). The British Chambers of Commerce (BCC) notes that its survey results across manufacturing and services are 'awful', the worst since the survey began in 1989: manufacturing, home sales and orders, employment expectations, investment, confidence, and cash flow have all hit record lows, and in the service sector every key area is at a new low (*BBC News* 13 January 2009). It is estimated that high street banks and other lenders sacked about 10,000 staff between October and December 2008, with tens of thousands of investment banking jobs having been cut by blue-chip companies such as Citigroup, Goldman Sachs, Morgan Stanley, and Deutsche Bank, as well as by the failure of Lehman Brothers. Up to 15,000 jobs in financial services are expected to be lost in the first few months of 2009 alone as levels of business plummet. Companies across the sector, from fund managers and insurers to high street banks and building societies, are planning to step up redundancy programmes. Tens of thousands of job losses in the next two years are expected by Lloyds TSB following its takeover of HBOS, and there are fears about the Royal Bank of Scotland, whose new chief executive is conducting a strategic review, with sharp cuts in staff numbers expected as a result (*Times* 12 January 2009).

The property market has continued its race from boom to bust. House prices have been falling since autumn 2007, and house sales have slumped by more than half in 2008 – causing the construction industry to plunge head-long into recession. House prices are expected to end the year 15 to 20 per cent lower than they started: the biggest annual slump on record. Most commentators believe that prices will continue falling well into 2009, and possibly for the whole of the year (*BBC News* 17 November 2008). Commercial property values have plunged by over 35 per cent from their peak 18 months previously, and are likely to finish down more than half by the end of 2009. This is expected to put further pressure on banks' balance sheets, and there is speculation as to a pending wave of property-firm failures (*Guardian* 16 January 2009). Repossessions have been rising: in the first three quarters of 2008 over 30,000 properties were repossessed, with predictions for the year 2008 of 45,000. An estimated 168,000 mortgage borrowers are at least three months in arrears on repayment, a figure which is being continuously revised upwards

(*Guardian* 21 November 2008). A £200mn mortgage rescue scheme is being rolled out across the whole of England by the UK government to try and stem the repossession crisis (*Guardian* 16 January 2009).

So far as current prospects for unemployment are concerned, the number of people out of work in the United Kingdom (around 1.92 mn in January 2009) is already reported to be at its highest level in more than a decade (*BBC News* 12 January 2009). The Confederation of British Industry (CBI) estimates that a further million people will join the jobless in 2009, taking the total to about three million (*Times* 12 January 2009). Interestingly, and according to a very recent survey by the British Trade Unions Congress (TUC), women are being made redundant at twice the rate of men (*BBC News* 21 January 2009). Recession and unemployment will have the usual knock on effects in the form of lowered tax receipts, increasing unemployment and associated benefit costs to government, and reduced consumer spending.

Portents and denials

The scale and threatened depth and persistence of this crisis in the United Kingdom raise certain questions, not least the state of denial preserved not only up to the nationalization of Northern Rock but even thereafter regarding weaknesses in the system. In this context, we argue that it is important to separate out proximate from underlying causes.

If the 'end of the party' in Britain – its poverty figures to one side – has been brought about initially by rising commodity prices and interest rates, in a context of a British property bubble waiting to burst, and capped moreover by 'the crisis in the financial system itself', with 'toxic derivatives' (Elliot and Atkinson 2008: 130–4), a freeze in inter-bank lending, and a credit crunch for both private businesses and consumers, then these might be seen as proximate causes from the viewpoint of economic failure. We can follow Elliot and Atkinson in noting that 'debt and delusion in the British economy' has played a major role in developments (ibid.: 158), as in the United States. And here it is important to distinguish underlying causes, as well as their manifestations. At one level, it is true that rising oil and food and other commodity prices were a global experience. It is also true that the United States suffered, like Britain, from a property bubble, and had moreover the first experience of the two countries with 'bursting', and with global implications: mortgage-backed securities – attracting a significant number of foreign investors – accounted for $6 trillion of $10 trillion's worth of mortgages outstanding, of which an unknown amount has been rendered 'toxic waste' (ibid.: 204–7). But the fact that Britain has also suffered from a property bubble is not thereby diminished: indeed, the UK housing market rose 'faster and further' than in America, with household balance sheets 'more stretched' (ibid.: 264; quoting Rob Camell of ING in London). In addition, both the US and UK bubbles were indelibly linked with experiments with financial deregulation, which should properly be viewed as policy decisions rather than as accidents.

In this respect, serious questions can be asked about the particular policies followed by New Labour, because it is these previous decisions which are reflected in today's major problems in the financial markets and in banking, and in exchange-rate volatility, and impacting negatively the real economy. In the context of the financial crisis, it is the case that New Labour continued with policies of financial deregulation begun under previous Conservative governments, including a permissive stance to Mrs Thatcher's abolition of foreign exchange controls, the foreign takeover of many British financial services businesses, the demutualization of building societies, the enticements to consumers to take out mortgages and loans, and to assumptions that the risk of bad debt could be readily managed. Moreover, the full independence granted to the Bank of England to set interest rates was 'the first big initiative of Tony Blair's government in May 1997' to 'strengthen the anti-inflation regime' (Elliot and Atkinson 2008: 118–23, 137), and serious questions again can be asked about the wisdom of this policy.

The nominal independence granted to the Bank of England was much lauded at the time by some policy commentators as an economic policy masterstroke by Gordon Brown. But in the absence of any other policy tools the only response in terms of Britain's macroeconomic management to the first impact of rising import prices of oil, food, and other commodities was to first increase and then maintain interest rates at a higher level than many considered wise – even after the housing bubble cracked and the financial crisis began to unfold. In fact, this stance continued almost until the end of 2007 when (on 20 December) 'a set of official statistics laid bare...the truly shocking state of the British economy' (Atkinson and Elliot

2008: 158). Even thereafter, when both businesses and consumers found that access to credit was drying up and borrowing conditions becoming difficult, the Bank proved slow to cut interest rates.[2] The view is now widely held that accolades given to the independence of the Bank played an invidious role in offering a sense of reassurance on the state of the economy where none was merited, and it is now a common argument that its policy remit was too narrowly focused. But it is equally true that the policy stance of New Labour reflected a willingness to assume that market economies are more or less self-adjusting, while its abrogation of interest rate responsibilities to an 'independent' Bank could also be construed as a political distancing from any desire to confront distributional questions in the economy – a point to which we return in the final chapter.

In any event, the stances taken on financial deregulation and debt and credit exposed weaknesses in the real economy – and hence in policy stances towards the real economy – even before the crisis hit. By late 2007, as 'easy credit' translated into a growing trade deficit in manufactures – an unresolved structural weakness highlighted by Elliot and Atkinson (2008: 171)[3] – current account deficits were hitting record levels. The surplus on services enjoyed by the United Kingdom comes nowhere near to matching the deficit on goods, and by late 2007 there was also a deficit on income from foreign investments, leading to the somewhat perverse situation where Britain (like America) was clearly borrowing from less developed countries (via sovereign wealth funds) (ibid.: 180–1, 209–14). This reflected both a weak internal manufacturing capability, and consumer spending fed by the illusion of wealth generated by a bubble economy. The total stock of individual debt in the shape of mortgages and consumer credit also hit record levels, totalling £1344 billion in June 2007 – 'broadly equivalent to one year's gross domestic product' (ibid.: 172). In fact, City analysts in the United Kingdom were predicting by late 2007 and in early 2008 that Britain 'could have a mini-perfect storm all of its own', with consumer profligacy giving way under a residential property crash, bankruptcies, and mortgage delinquencies – in a context of a constrained Bank of England and rising government budget deficits (ibid.: 264–5).

Given these circumstances, there are compelling reasons to think that particular policy stances in Britain have both contributed to the crisis and rendered it particularly vulnerable, notwithstanding US parallels and the worldwide impacts of commodity price shifts. The most recent International Monetary Fund (IMF) forecast – released on 28 January 2009 – predicts not only that British GDP will shrink by nearly 3 per cent in the current year, but that Britain's economy is the most vulnerable amongst the world's economies, the general forecast being in the order of a 2 per cent shrinkage for 'advanced nations' as a whole.[4] This latest prediction repeats previous warnings that Britain is *especially* vulnerable to recession for reasons including the behaviour of its housing market, while going further than before in downgrading in particular UK growth forecasts within a generally deteriorating situation.

The paradox in this context, and despite the evidence of particular problems for the United Kingdom, is the tendency in some press and political commentary, even where policy failings are acknowledged, to view the United States, or even a 'global crisis', as the primary culprit. While to some extent explicable by America's size and global significance, and by the worldwide reach of the crisis, this leaves the impression that the United Kingdom is a smaller culprit. This has undoubtedly enabled an interesting element of political spin. Thus, Gordon Brown has made consistent references to the global crisis (see also, with respect to his speech in 1999 on economic fears in 1997–1998, Elliot and Atkinson [2008: 173–4]), and to the problems emanating from the United States (ibid.: 264). For example, when asked about David Cameron's criticism of his conduct of UK economic policy, Brown's response has been that his 'undivided attention is on taking this country through the difficult times as a result of a global problem that started in America' (see *Guardian* 17 October 2008). This has translated into a situation where claims are entertained that Britain is leading the world in the particular policy shifts and responses to crisis – 'saving the world' rather than 'sinking it'.[5] Gordon Brown's immediate response in parliament to the most recent and downgraded IMF report has been more of the same, referencing both the US and global economy, and Britain's lead in responding.

But what the press is now dubbing a 'new' or 'second' banking crisis makes it clear that the crisis is far from over: renewed worries of a secondary banking collapse in the United States following (in January 2009) Washington's emergency $140 bn rescue package for Bank of America, and concerns for Citigroup, have been quickly reflected in sharp falls in banking shares in the City as fears grow that UK banks like Barclays and Royal Bank of Scotland have greater problems than already exposed. This has prompted the prime minister, chancellor, and governor of the Bank of England to meet to compile another emergency package to shore up the banking system and get credit moving through the economy (*Independent* 18 January 2009). In a typically interesting commentary on monetary matters, Will Hutton observes that banking systems of some countries are now suffering because of Britain's exploded bubble, while at the same time its own property crisis and credit crunch has been exacerbated because foreign banks and foreign capital have supported up to a third of all UK lending – and have gone bust or fled. As he puts it, Britain's banks are in no position to plug the gap so the UK government has to 'put the system back together with a weak, non-reserve currency'. Hutton argues that, compared with the United States:

> Britain, by contrast, has not begun to mobilise on anything like the same scale – even though in many respects our crisis is more acute. Barclays, for example, is in a position analogous to Citigroup and Bank of America. In 2007 close to half its profits came from 'investment banking', now so perilous for its American counterparts. Barclays is the leader in so-called corporate 'synthetic' structured investment vehicles – complex and even more dodgy than the securities that have brought low Citigroup and Bank of America.... Unless we act quickly, decisively and cleverly, the difficulties of our banks could overwhelm us, triggering an enormous run on the pound. Britain, in short, risks bankruptcy'.
> (Hutton 2009)

The end of things: responses to crisis

There is little doubt but that there is considerable potential for public anger, or even social tension, in the United Kingdom as well as other affected countries, given the circumstances of the crisis.[6] The sight of senior bank employees awarding themselves millions after having nearly bankrupted the financial and economic system, and the prospect of more government bail outs at the risk of billions in taxpayers' money has grated. To electorates and populations fed a steady diet of preaching about unstoppable globalization and the powerlessness of states, the spectacle of not only banks but also global auto companies and other private firms seeking state assistance[7] may prove an important corrective. Although prediction is always hazardous, responses are likely to harden further as job losses and dependence on benefits grow, and as cuts in hours and wages – already being imposed by or negotiated with some UK employers, some of whom may well be acting opportunistically – proceed. Moreover, the loss of incomes from savings as interest rates plummet in an attempt to stimulate spending (devastating to some pensioners who have been encouraged to 'save for their old age', and of little demonstrated impact to date on either bank lending or consumer expenditure), the impact on consumer psychology of negative equity, and the realities of personal indebtedness as the ability to pay off debt disappears – all are likely to create or heighten feelings of alienation within a deeply inequitable system, and to provoke responses. All are likely to add to the increased pressure of inequality and poverty in Britain. How this translates into electoral and other pressures is, of course, an open question.

Paradoxically, while events compel a de facto questioning of economic systems and priorities, in Britain the policy response has lagged consistently behind. For example, Gordon Brown has stressed the need for G7 countries to sustain demand, and for more intergovernmental oversight of financial systems internationally, but despite some perhaps premature speculation that this constitutes a return to 'Keynesian' demand management, there has actually been little radical overhaul to date. Nobody has been keener than Brown, prior to the banking crisis, in arguing for open markets and tough anti-inflationary policies based on simple policy rules – and 'key to this is the notion that markets will become less volatile if they can only be made more transparent' (see Elliott and Atkinson 2008: 280–1). At the start of 2009, Gordon Brown also announced intentions to create 100,000 jobs through demand-side measures: but this also cannot be regarded as realized evidence of a radical policy shift. And where nationalizations or bail outs have occurred in the United Kingdom – as in the United States – these have tended to be cast by policy-makers as 'temporary' aberrations in order to restore the operation of free markets. Indeed, recently announced plans to push privatization further in the British Post Office may have been introduced partly with 'reassurance' in mind. It may be the case too that

New Labour will suffer from its ideological baggage, and an intellectual endowment totally unprepared for what is now a 'crisis-in-being', rather than, as previously, a 'crisis-in-waiting', anticipated without and discounted within.

Even if the British public does not lay blame at the door of a New Labour project now enjoying a third term in government vis-à-vis the dispositions of the party leadership, and over a period in which some at least of the fundamental problems with the British economy were already visible or clearly emerging, the early murmurs (including Will Hutton) that its policy responses are not brave enough may intensify. Whether the Labour Party leadership will be able to step beyond its confines to put together a coherent and entirely alternative new policy agenda in time for an imminent general election will be the key issue ahead of it. Ironically, and notwithstanding the palpable differences in much of the structure of their economies and the newly discovered tendency of New Labour to blame the United States for its present difficulties, much may also depend upon the extent to which the new American president, Barack Obama, is willing or able to set out a fresh economic agenda that marks a genuine break from the mindsets and policies of recent decades, and enjoys wider global influence.[8]

The 'credit crunch' is generating a rapidly growing press and literature. Academic debate, for all the usual reasons, can only follow with something of a lag. A question, however, pertains to the nature of the debate to be held; and in particular whether the crisis will lead to a systemic and deep reappraisal of markets and market failures. Some contributions, questioning the way in which transnational corporations and 'globalization' are viewed as agencies superseding nation states, call for reinvigorated state-promoted institutions at both the national and pan-national level to provide controls. Elliott and Atkinson (2008), influenced by Roosevelt and Atlee, also call for reinvigorated social welfare programmes and 'a interventionist and reflationary economic policy', and something more akin to continental social democracy (ibid.: 286–98). Robert Reich (2008) calls for strengthened democracy and democratic forms, arguing that 'the triumph of supercapitalism [Reich's term] has led, indirectly and unwittingly, to the decline of democracy', as well as widening inequality (ibid.: 224; also 209–24). Coming from very diverse political positions, the economist Irwin Stelzer argues that 'the day when that engine of capitalism, the financial market, will be allowed to operate more or less unimpeded by government, has passed ... capitalism as we have known it is no more ... a New Capitalism is in the process of creation ...' (*Guardian* 26 September 2008), while Joseph Stiglitz argues that the crisis 'is the fruit of a pattern of dishonesty on the part of financial institutions, and incompetence on the part of policymakers' (*Guardian* 16 September 2008), with belief in minimal government and self-adjusting markets a major policy error.

Summing up

What is eminently clear is that no summing up at this stage is possible beyond the obvious that much has changed, and that more change can be expected. At a relatively early stage in the recession, one that may prove severe and prolonged, pressures will mount that could cumulatively stimulate a broadening of debate as to what has gone wrong, encouraging a more systematic reappraisal of developments than has yet been engaged in by most politicians, and certainly those laying claim to status in 'New Labour'. In recounting the appearance of crisis, we have presented developments in a way which reflects the speed and drama of its unfolding, before an afflicted electorate. We have also emphasized both the denial of portents, and the eschewing of responsibilities, on the part of the New Labour government, while also recognizing its inherited problems. While care should always be taken when referencing Anglo-American capitalism, given the manifest economic and social differences between Britain and the United States, the changed status of the latter in New Labour rhetoric on the crisis – a hero gone to zero – is one of the more ironic features of its response to the realities of a downturn long brewing. Any suggestion that Britain has somehow been, at worse, a junior partner in organizing the conditions of the crisis now impacting upon it, is far from being credible. Important questions also arise for existing forms of academic analysis of both the New Labour project as such, and varieties of capitalism more generally – to this we now turn.

8
Strange Days

In this book we have broached capitalism as it exists in Britain today by considering aspects of the British state as it displays itself in various guises – responding to an unwelcome decision by a large and mobile transnational corporation, attempting to build public services provision while simultaneously shrinking state organization, and seeking to claim the status of model employer while presiding over entrenched structures of material inequality and gendered disadvantages in its own workforce – and via a commentary on aspects of each of two major policy themes, Thatcherism and New Labour. Our approach throughout takes a particular turn, because while certainly interested in the purely empirical side of things we are also concerned at every stage with questions of legitimation and denial, and the gaps evident between policy rhetoric and realities. While by no means intended or presented as an exhaustive treatment or coverage of issues, our starting point in this regard is with an alternative perspective on the comparative extent to which Britain within Europe experienced industrial difficulties at the end of the long boom following the Second World War, within which to sketch an alternative understanding of the later shocks of the Thatcher period and the implications of the policy conversions evident in the New Labour project – brought into sharp relief by the latest economic and financial crisis to engulf Britain.

Strange days are here

Even before the current economic crisis, the fact of a post-Soviet world and the coincident loss of confidence in socialist projects in the West brought with it many oddly nuanced reactions to and reflections upon what remains. Geoff Harcourt, a great Cambridge economist of the 'old school', has recently drawn attention to an address delivered by Paul Samuelson to the Bank of Italy in 1997, the year that saw the election of the first Blair-led Labour party government in the United Kingdom. Samuelson, awarded the economist's version of the Nobel Prize, while possessed not only of an exceptional mathematical facility but also a generally humane disposition, is nonetheless known to be averse to political positions departing from his own notional centre – and perhaps most markedly so for those departing to the left. In his address, however, Samuelson touched on ways in which America's model of capitalism differs from the 'European': 'In America we now operate...the Ruthless Economy...we now have a Cowed Labor Force...two features...interrelated...[yet]...somewhat indistinguishable' (Samuelson 1997: 6–7; cited in Harcourt 2006: 127). Coming from Samuelson, these are unexpected associations. Indeed, like many academic writers professing an aversion to left-facing radicalism, Samuelson's career output includes a definite, if rather negative, absorption with Karl Marx. As Professor Harcourt playfully observes, 'Karl, that you should have lived to see this hour' (Harcourt 2006: ibid.).

In Britain itself, a similar blurring of sensibilities has been evident. A decade on, 'Red' Ken Livingstone, a significant figure on the British political left for many years, and writing as the still incumbent Mayor of London approaching the end of a second term in office, can be found declaring his intent to use elbows and knees to capitalize on London's comparative strength as a world city, reflecting both its cosmopolitanism – its willingness to embrace 'internationalisation like no other city – understanding it not only as an economic but [also] a social and cultural process' (Livingstone 2007: 1) – but also the advantages afforded it by a permissive 'financial regulatory regime':

> From London's financial regulatory regime, through to the fact that over 60 per cent of Londoners are born outside the city, to its determinedly multicultural character, London has pushed ahead on internationalisation while other cities have hesitated...(Livingstone 2007: page 1 of 2)

If for the more conservative US economist Paul Samuelson the world was developing not quite as expected, for the radical Mayor of London there is no alternative but to seek local advantages in the competitive environment forged by global capitalism. Yet at the same time, Ken Livingstone declares himself an unrepentant socialist still

> one day the idea that the main means of production are owned by private individuals or that one person who owns capital can decide to sack 100,000 who contribute their work, will be considered as anti-democratic as the idea serfs could be tied to the land. But I will not be alive when that day comes. (Livingstone 2007: ibid.)

although radical change, while still inevitable, now sits beyond life's expectation.

We live in strange days. But if it is interesting to contrast the perturbed moderate conservative confronted with some of the implications of untrammelled capitalism with the more complex juxtapositioning of aspirations and opportunities evident in the ruminations of a socialist, the oddness of the times become more apparent still when we consider the absence of any trace of unsettled thought in the policy formulations which have dominated government in both the United States and Britain in recent years, and not only from the self-acknowledged right wing of the political spectrum. In the British case, the terms of reference of the New Labour project have implied nothing but a curt dismissal of the issues raised by Samuelson, contempt for the hopes of socialists. Theorized as a 'third way', restricted in its ambitions, and locked in a state of denial and legitimation that may or may not be finally exploded by the unravelling of a debt-ridden economy, the uncertainty of the times and the widely felt dissatisfactions with the world as it exists have been more or less completely dismissed – at least up until the present crisis.

Our concern has therefore been with questions of legitimation and denial, and gaps between policy rhetoric and realities, for their own sake, and as a means by which to better understand the juncture at which the British variety of capitalism now finds itself.

Legitimation and denial: shocks and conformity

Our starting point, however, has been with the shock years of the 1980s, and the onslaught orchestrated by Mrs Thatcher's Conservative party governments against the position of organized labour in the British economy. We propose that the political development now forever known as 'Thatcherism' is best understood if due scope is given to its contingent and opportunistic features. Building on an existing body of research work – associated in the United Kingdom principally with Keith Cowling – we have suggested that Britain's economy was destabilized in the 1970s as a consequence of the aggressive profit-seeking actions of (principally) manufacturing corporations seeking to further develop Europe as a regional theatre of operations; and that this process of de-industrialization was then exacerbated by policies enacted under Mrs Thatcher in the context of a fierce reaction scapegoating Britain's trade unions. We thereby sketch both an enriched context in which to locate and consider the recent and controversial thesis advanced by Naomi Klein (2007) concerning the role of economic instability in advancing the policy agendas of radical right governments adopting shock tactics as this applies to Britain, and also the outlines of an alternative take on its recent economic and political history, moving from Thatcherism through to New Labour. The earlier weakening of the British trade union movement, for over a decade now in the oxymoronic position of being a principal source of Labour party funds and a publicly sidelined policy influence, is widely recognized as having been integral to the degree of freedom accorded the New Labour project under Tony Blair and Gordon Brown, and its politically contingent and opportunistic features.

On a substantial range of policy issues New Labour's practical concessions to the stances adopted by the previous Conservative party governments of Margaret Thatcher and John Major have been marked, at least prior to the still unfolding but totally unpredicted economic and financial crisis – favouring weak unions and deregulated markets, and conceding unreservedly to the view that private sector management is intrinsically more effective than public, even in the organization of public services delivery.

This bigger picture is important. James Galbraith, son of the late John Kenneth, and a formidable economist in his own right, has recently recommended that critical economists develop the skill of *explication de texte* – 'the deconstruction ... of official statements' – as a promising means of transforming policy conduct, on grounds that public policy figures, if unmoved by mere matters of evidence, may nonetheless prove susceptible to public embarrassment when confronted by the 'elementary illogic' evident in their 'verbal exposition' of policy matters (Galbraith 2005: 21). But what strikes one at least as much as the manifestations of elementary illogic in the official policy positions which we have encountered in the course of this book, is how impervious to criticism the conduct of economic policy formulation by New Labour has typically been. While no doubt sustained by a large parliamentary majority and a Conservative opposition unwilling to attack its policies on markets, unions, and private sector management, to fully understand what has inoculated official policy against embarrassment we must also consider the forms of legitimation adopted against the awkward facts denied – to be interpreted in the light of previous shocks to Britain's political economy.

Thus, the first of our three case examples deals with the production politics of competitiveness when a government commits itself to maintaining a porous economy with the purpose of rendering it attractive to mobile corporations. The circumstances surrounding our case example – a Ford factory closure – point to the outlines of a tacit bargaining game enacted under conditions in which a transnational producer distributes work across multiple sites separated by national borders, and as such there are interesting technical aspects to the case which warrant some consideration.[1] Our main concern, however, is with responses to an embarrassing corporate decision, in which responses both legitimation and denial are active and present. A 'good' reason is found for a regrettable factory closure, amidst much contrary evidence; a boast is delivered as to the advantages of an existing policy stance, regardless of a poor national employment and trade performance in cars as in other branches of manufacturing activity. If the forms of legitimation are clumsy – recall the official declaration that UK-based auto manufacture is the 'leanest' in the EU, if amongst the least productive – we have also argued that the previous state of dependency to which Britain has been reduced with respect to the investment decisions of transnational producers provides the relevant context for interpretation.

Similarly, the second of our case examples, exploring the boundaries between the state and the private sector in the organization of public sector services, raises points of independent interest. The Private Finance Initiative (PFI) appears quite remarkable if considered as an experiment designed to test just how far a state committed to expanding the private sector will go in declaring its own organizational incompetence. Here, the forms of legitimation, as embodied in Treasury procedures regulating awards to private sector consortiums contracted to finance and organize capital projects and to provide services, are more subtle: as we have seen, the bias against public sector organization admitted to under the 'rules' is smaller than the bias the 'rules' hide away. Denial that this is so has been less subtle – recall Allyson Pollock's remark that when confronted by concerns about the rules governing PFI awards Gordon Brown simply intoned that the public sector was bad at management, the private sector good[2] – but again interpretation is best made in the light of previous developments and earlier privatizations.

The third of our case examples is the most complex because when we turn to the state in its guise as a major employer of workers we encounter historically inherited and deeply entrenched systems of inequality and material disadvantage predating both the election of the first of the New Labour governments and also its Conservative predecessors. The self-declared status of the British state as a 'model' or 'good' employer is rich both in assumed moral authority – an act of nuanced and temporally contingent legitimation – and of denials of fact. As we have shown, employment in the UK state sector is characterized by endemic problems not only of low pay but also of unequal pay, with a large and persistent gender pay gap. To contrast rhetoric with reality in this instance is important for many reasons, and not least to demonstrate that the state is not 'a witness apart' to discriminatory practices in the private sector, to be moved (or not) to take legislative measures to intervene. The imperative of restraining wage costs in the state sector necessarily affects the regulation of terms of conditions and employment more generally, including the size of the minimum wage. Promises to advance workplace equalities must be squared against the contrary pressures of 'liberalization' (including outsourcing and privatization), which frequently involves bypassing trade unions and undermining workers' conditions. In practice, little is likely to be gained by the mass of women workers unless the state's own employment practices are addressed, but the potentially large implications for tax and spending structures of a kind that British governments have consistently shied away from militate against change. The borderline between legitimation and self-deception is no more blurred than here.

From a methodological perspective the different guises in which the state presents itself as policy maker offer avenues of exploration by which to begin to address the difficult question of the state's general character, vis-à-vis the variety of 'its' capitalism. That all governments can obfuscate is demonstrated by our 'model employer' study. But an interesting question to consider is the extent to which for New Labour practical policy conversion – on a range of key issues – to essentially Thatcherite themes reflects a real intellectual conversion as opposed to a purely pragmatic response to an inherited condition, a mere empirical acceptance of the 'world as it is'. We have noted the narrowing of ambitions of New Labour in government, described in depth by David Coates, although this in itself could be interpreted in different ways. But we have also observed the easy way in which Giddens' theorization of the third way, a study in denial and a substantial legitimizing project in its own right, elides into an assumption that the crisis of capitalism before Thatcherism was in fact socialism's last gasp. And at every stage the details of our case examples suggest something active as well as passive.

Were we able to halt at this point our final conclusion inasmuch as New Labour is concerned would be that the game being played in Britain today – 'Britain's' variety of capitalism – has deep and complex roots, but a finite and rapidly shortening life. The exploding of the housing market bubble and the near collapse of a deregulated financial system has irrevocably punctured any illusion of economic success. The manufacturing base is once again shrinking, at its fastest rate since the policy-enhanced recession ushered in by the monetarist policies of Mrs Thatcher almost thirty years ago. PFI is in danger of imminent collapse as firms struggle to raise finance, and in a context where a far smaller investment has been made in public infrastructure in exchange for future state spending commitments than would have been possible without the scheme. It is hard not to see a prospective squeeze on public sector spending – notwithstanding press speculation about the rediscovered 'Keynesianism' of New Labour – impacting heavily on public sector workers, with negative implications for low pay and equalities. Poorer groups, well represented in Britain today, are again also likely to be amongst the hardest hit. It is perhaps ironic that the response thus far has involved further layers of denial, legitimation, and 'elementary illogic', not least in the form of claims that the crisis started elsewhere while the United Kingdom is leading the way out of it.

Globalization and the varieties of capitalism debate

As a contribution to the broader varieties of capitalism debate, our approach is consistent with the historically oriented conceptualization of David Coates, grounded in a sense of the tensions within capitalist economies and also the interaction between capitalist economies as these inform empirically observed propensities towards crisis and change. Our specific views on the Klein 'shock' thesis, and a non-linear interpretation of the path followed from the economic stresses of the 1970s through to Thatcherism and New Labour, while raising many points for further study – on the side of 'capital', for example, and on the question of the balance and global positioning of class-forces, a fuller account would have to distinguish between the role of large and small businesses in driving developments and the experiences of property rights holders in each – is nonetheless a thesis that could only be developed via this kind of approach. At the same time, we attach a great deal of weight to a close study of forms of legitimation and denial, themes that could be further developed not only in relation to particular state policy platforms, as illustrated in our case examples, but also in relation to this thesis.

For this reason, we should be wary of explanatory frameworks, however radically framed or intended, which rationalize authority structures. In this category we might include, and for the reasons discussed in this book, the sort of simple profit squeeze hypothesis that argues that the crisis of capitalism at the end of the long boom after the Second World War simply reflected pressures of international competition on the one hand, and the strength of organized labour on the other, an empirically unconvincing thesis that grows weaker the more countries it includes. In the same category, and in many ways far more interesting to consider, is the attempt to explain the end of the long boom as a transitionary process from a Fordist to a post-Fordist world. The inversions used to contrast 'Fordist' with 'post-Fordist' production systems are more often than not historical and empirical bunk, as with the inaccurate dating of the appearance of flexible assembly systems and custom building in the Western car industry; and when these inversions are then brought together as 'packaged contrasts' functional associations can be invented where none in fact exist, and certainly not in the prescribed manner.[3] By the same token, although by its nature this is always a risk in any comparative work, we should be wary of overly dramatized accounts of a fundamental shift in relations of production and (or) consumption as one variety of capitalism encounters another. Here we can think of the use made of 'Japanese' manufacturing practices both in the literatures developing a post-Fordism theme, and in Western accounts of 'lean production'.[4]

Industrial symbols and their political constructs are important more generally, but also potentially very misleading, and again we should be wary. For example, we have argued that Britain suffered economically to the extent that it did in the 1970s, following on from the end of long boom after the Second World War, not because of the weakness of its large corporations within Europe, but rather because of their profit-seeking propensities. One notable exception, however, was the ill-fated British Leyland, a British-owned giant founded in the run-up to EEC entry on the 'national champion' model. In the same way that Klein argues that Thatcherism 'parlayed' economic difficulties into the opportunity for a radical capitalist revolution in the 1980s, further research is needed on the ways in which the particular experience of British Leyland was constructed and generalized as a symbol of industrial decline, of the failures of state led restructuring and nationalization – the struggling British Leyland was brought into public ownership before Mrs Thatcher privatized it[5] – and evidence of the 'hooligan' nature of British trade unions.

Our approach is thus one that opts for a historically rooted approach, seeking to avoid the dangers of overly linear and overly rationalized readings of developments. We make the case accordingly for giving due scope to political opportunism as well as agency – albeit within historically structured contexts[6] – as an independent factor, of relevance to the study both of Thatcherism and of its successor development, in New Labour.

For the same reason that we are attracted to the general stance suggested by Coates, we reject the narrower VoC framework as conceived by Hall and Soskice. Not only is it simply impossible to frame the sort of issues with which we have been concerned in this book within the conceptual framework they provide, but that framework itself can easily be construed as a legitimizing construct. While there is no need to labour this point, a recent application of the VoC framework to the British case in terms of the developments leading up to and through the Thatcher era seems principally to argue that the British

labour movement was a 'major impediment' to the control of inflation in the 1970s, while generating high levels of industrial conflict,
a problem not helped by the 'weakness of British employers associations' (see Hall 2007: 53–4). Mrs Thatcher is then credited with seeing to the problem by stoking the fires of competition. Indeed, the
general sense in this instance is that European economies not organized on the British model need intellectual reassurance and support,
given the latter's 'comparative advantages': 'not surprisingly, rates of
growth of employment and national product have been higher in
Britain than in France or Germany' (ibid.: 66–7). It does not look
so good now. As we have previously observed, some frameworks are
more of their time than others are.

One last point is worth making. One feature of the VoC literature,
very much in evidence in the application of it to the British case just
cited, is that deregulated and weakly unionized labour markets have
served to eliminate problems of inflation caused by high (money)
wage settlements feeding through to higher prices. But doubts have
recently been expressed as to whether Britain's 'inflation problem'
has in fact disappeared. For example, in his recent study Wilkinson
(2007: 831–5) argues that British inflation rates have been sensitive
'since the 1960s' to the sterling price of imports; and we have described
how the only response available to the Bank of England to the recent
spikes in the import prices of oil, food, and other commodities was
to raise interest rates. It seems likely that had the pressure of rising
import prices not abated, the strength of the macroeconomic regime
in Britain – even with deregulated labour markets bolstered by a large
increase in the employment of migrant workers[7] – would have been
severely tested, both on the economic front and on the political. In
this scenario, the failure of New Labour to engage directly with distributional issues in the economy might in any case have appeared
increasingly as a failure of state planning. Since over the longer term
there is no reason to suppose that world oil prices (at least) will not
rise again, after the price-depressing effects of the recession pass, this
issue will return.

Summing up

If we ask what variety of capitalism British capitalism is then the most
reasonable short answer would have to be that it is a very complex

one. But the juncture at which Britain's variety of capitalism now finds itself can be at least partially grasped by an assessment of the different policy stances of New Labour in office. We need not repeat the obvious, namely that New Labour differs from Thatcherism as well as from 'old' Labour, although we have proposed that it is all but impossible to understand New Labour without an appreciation of the 'shocks' to which Britain was previously subjected by Mrs Thatcher's governments, including the active suppression of its trade union movement. Both observations stand as correctives to the view that 'states' are passively locked into the policies they pursue as a consequence of the variety of capitalism they inhabit. However, at the same time the confluence of circumstances giving birth to New Labour appear increasingly to have produced a product mainly novel for its abject features. Limited policy objectives have been pursued with mixed results; a wider neglect of real but difficult issues like productivity, investment, and income distribution masked by an illusion of success sustained only by unsustainable debt; and a lack of ambition throughout reflected in a contrary rhetoric and practice, and 'elementary illogic'. Here we can only repeat Coates' observation that the United Kingdom has managed to sit somewhere between America and Europe, while scoring poorly on both comparisons. The British variety of capitalism may therefore be a complex one, but it is not impressive.

Throughout its periods in office, New Labour has been active in its advocacy of market liberalization, of free capital movements, of weak protection for workers, and of the prerogatives of profit-seeking businesses. As we have observed at several junctures in this book, to interpret the 'global' as the active but alien and external presence, and the nation state as passive, would be naïve. But at the same time, and throughout the same period, New Labour has repeatedly invoked global forces in a manner implying something separate and apart – 'exogenous' – determining as if on the basis of some inexorable logic the manner in which capitalism must work, with minimal regulation and interference from either state or supra-state bodies. This policy attitude has left Britain particularly vulnerable as its contradictions emerge in full, so it is perhaps unsurprising that the 'crisis' is also to be treated as an exogenous event as government representatives engage in new forms of legitimation and denial. An interesting question at the point of writing is whether the electorate in the United Kingdom will find this credible.

Notes

1 Introduction

1. Britain's status as an island is said in this instance to have shielded it through the sixteenth and seventeenth centuries (up until England's Civil War) from the damaging effects of the 'almost constant warfare' on the Continent; of huge importance, according to this writer, to its internal development (Hill 2002: 15). While we shall not be going quite so far back in time in the present book, it is perhaps salutary to remember that Britain took a divergent path from the rest of Europe at a very early stage in its development as a capitalist economy: shielded from one type of exposure, it went on to develop – a global commercial and industrial empire.
2. We touch upon some of Giddens' views, as indeed those of other writers mentioned in this introduction – at various points in this book.
3. Coates' (2000) *Models of Capitalism*, a comparative survey of Anglo-American, Japanese, German, and Swedish economic models, is a model example of a contribution to the varieties of capitalism literature with a rich and expansive purview of issues.
4. We should perhaps acknowledge E.P. Thompson (1993) for this analogy. We touch on some reasons for the de-gendering of the varieties of capitalism debate in this book.

2 Globalization and Capitalism Unleashed: The Travails of Labour

1. Developments were not of course identical everywhere: Japan, in particular, has only relatively recently begun to experience something like Thatcherism, and then only in the context of the sustained length of the long downturn that commenced in the early 1990s. Some valuable contextualization in this connection is provided in Werner (2007) (see also Coates 2007).
2. That monetarism was a reversion to the incomes policy of Karl Marx has become a much repeated quip since.
3. The official unemployment rate as measured by the UK 'claimant count' (those entitled to receive benefits as unemployed workers) rose from 5.3 per cent in 1979, the year of Mrs Thatcher's election, to over 10 per cent in 1981, where it stayed until 1988. But the sharp rise in this measure of unemployment was accompanied by a series of downward revisions based on administrative changes as to who was eligible for inclusion, so a peak year is hard to identify. For example, in 1984 a rate of 13.1 per cent was reported, but only in that year. The now preferred and ILO endorsed Labour Force Survey (LFS) measure used by today's government is calculated from a household survey

of the number of individuals seeking work but not in a job: in every year since this has become available, it has tracked above the official claimant count.

4. On the question of whether the corporate sector in the 1970s was subjected to a profit squeeze resulting from trade union pressure combined with international competition, the evidence relied upon by Glyn (2006) refers back to a much earlier study by Glyn and Sutcliffe (1972). This was rejected empirically by Cowling (1982: see especially chapter 6), who also offered a quite different explanation of the economic downturn at the end of the long boom, and included the thesis that the problem was not one of *excessive* wages for workers but rather one of inadequate consumption potentials *from* wages, even if fully expended, vis-à-vis industrial capacity.

5. Since the Singh test is prominent in the UK de-industrialization debate (the same key passage is cited, for example, in Rowthorn and Wells (1987: 232), a major survey), we should perhaps briefly note here Paul Krugman's (1994) challenge to this kind of definition; this was made in response to Laura Tyson's later but very similar definition of the issue for the United States – that it should 'meet the test of international competition' while generating 'sustainable' increases in the domestic standard of living (see Tyson 1992, cited in Krugman 1994: 31–32). Krugman simply dismisses the issue: the 'world's leading nations' are not 'to any important degree in economic competition', nor can their 'major economic problems be attributed to failures to compete on world markets' (Krugman 1994: 30). And to establish this point as a general principle he compares, for the United States, movements in domestic rates of productivity growth with movements in the terms of trade (ibid.: 32), and claims that the former rather than the latter accounted for the weak performance of America in the 1970s and 1980s. But this is not compelling: it is a mistake to suppose that domestic rates of productivity growth are self-evidently determined separately from performance in trade, for reasons we discuss. Moreover, generalizations beyond the United States, far more closed than the United Kingdom, are problematic.

6. In the relatively brief period when UK macroeconomic policy was 'officially monetarist', this kind of fear was dismissed, on grounds that inflation is driven by the money supply not money wage settlements and price-setting decisions of firms. This view did not persist long.

7. In their otherwise fine reply to Krugman (1994) (see note 5 above) Howes and Singh (2000) overlook the importance of this distinction: following Kaldor – for example, Kaldor (1978) – they emphasize the firm as the unit of competition, but assume that it is nationally rooted (see also Coffey and Thornley, 2007).

8. For example, while GKN in fierce competition with Bosch and other interests in Germany acquired facilities in the (relatively) low strike Germany, Lucas made acquisitions in France and Italy and Spain; Associated Engineering also made acquisitions in France and Italy as well as Germany; and so forth (see Bhaskar 1979: 304–318). US firms, long active in British-based auto sector components, were better represented in the commercial vehicles sections of the industry at this time – they similarly expanded towards Europe.

9. With British car makers indicating that 'some 55 per cent of the total ex-works cost of their products' was bought out from suppliers, far higher than was the case for most European car makers, and with 'cost advantages of up to 27 per cent' reported for UK component makers (see Bhaskar 1979: 303; 306–07), something more than a tale of British inefficiency is needed to explain what happened to the ill-starred British Leyland Motor Corporation. It is worth noting that as Britain went into Europe both Ford *and* the big British component part suppliers adopted far more aggressive postures towards British Leyland. On the relationship between British-owned car assembly and the conduct of British part suppliers, Cowling observes as follows: 'The 'British' part of the British motor industry...a small group of powerful...components manufacturers being supplied with assembly services at or *below* competitive rates by an independent downstream assembler (BL)...unprofitable, partly as a result of their [suppliers'] own activities...[as these suppliers] *switched their production* to a Continental EEC base...[this] allowed BL gradually to be run down' (Cowling 1986: 34; emphasis added).

10. The literature here is enormous. Foreign direct investment (FDI) registers in econometric studies as sensitive to international wage differences (see, for example, Tomlinson (2002) for a good representative study, focusing on Japanese FDI); consistently, domestic investment rates also register as increasingly sensitive to relative labour costs (Hatzius (2000), explores the implications for worker's bargaining in the United Kingdom and Germany); controlling an international division of labour also appears to be a motivating factor for transnationals (Peoples and Sugden (2000) review case study and other evidence for the United Kingdom and the United States); and so forth. A simple formal literature also exists exploring these themes (for example, Huizinga 1990). But in addition to this specific economics literature, the point is more generally accepted that 'one of the most important aspects' of foreign direct investment is the advantages it gives transnational corporations when bargaining with workers (see Glyn 2006: 101; also chapter 5).

11. As to why Britain should prove so vulnerable to the destabilizing conduct of the firms it was hosting as the European market was extended and consolidated, this remains an area with rich resource potential. One could note, for example, Reich's (1990) study of the different and historically and globally specific trajectories of state attitudes to industry in Britain and Germany over the middle part of the twentieth century, and the eventual impact on how Ford Motor Company came to orient itself in relation to Europe. As evident from Tony Benn's diaries, the British government can scarcely be said to have been consulted as Ford prepared to change its stance, in the later 1960s: 'Ford had decided to try to build up a European Ford instead of basing itself on individual companies, like Ford of Britain or Ford of Germany...[the Ford executive said] 'I thought I'd tell you as a courtesy'. I was amazed' (Benn 1987: 504). We explore some consequences of this in Chapter 3, with a case study of a Ford factory closure in Britain.

12. The 'othering' of Japan has been widely discussed in connection with changing Western forms of discourse over trade with the Asia Pacific (see, for example, Ngai-Ling Sum, 2000). One complicating issue is the role played by the Japanese firm Toyota in myth-making about Japanese achievements in the auto and other manufacturing industries – a complex topic, and one touched upon at various junctures in Coffey (2006). For example, Taichii Ohno, who finished up as an executive vice president of Toyota, wrote a book for Japanese audiences in the 1970s boasting about how the company had now surpassed Henry Ford by mixing model specifications on a single assembly line (see ibid.: 38, and note 16 thereto) – for many decades by that point a standard Western practice. The nuances of how one interprets this kind of boasting in its Japanese context are complex, even before considering the efforts of post-Fordists. But on these latter efforts at least some clear judgements are possible: insofar as 'Japanese' production systems are concerned, many of the claims in works like Best (1990) ('the new competition') or Lash and Urry (1994) ('reflexive accumulation') are counterfactual in their assumptions.

13. A relevant discussion of the issues on vertical ownership in control vis-à-vis comparison between Japanese and Western automakers is also given in Coffey and Tomlinson (2003): the key point is that on some measures firms like Toyota or Nissan in the 1980s were very well integrated vertically, acknowledgement of which disappeared rapidly in this decade.

14. For example, Buechler (2000) argues (like Glyn) that 'by the mid-1970s, it was evident that international competition and the relatively high cost of US labour were creating new problems of accumulation for US capital', with a response which entailed 'a ragged but progressive dismantling of the Fordist structure'. We have already (see note 4) listed some objections. So far as *international competition* and *labour* costs for the United States are concerned, we might also note that while American hourly compensation rates were flat (and wage bills starting to tumble as work was outsourced to de-unionized sites) the US trade deficit with Japan increased anyway, even though Japanese hourly compensation rates were rising (see, for instance, the various discussions in Mann 2000: 79–80; Luria 2000; Howes and Singh 2000: 4). The details of the evidence paint a far more complex picture than Buechler suggests. A more general kind of claim that 'Fordism' implied some kind of *balance* between production potentials and realized consumption, and that this then broke down, is equally unappealing: as should be clear from today's economic crises, imbalances developed *over* the boom period.

3 The Commanding State: The Politics of Competitiveness

1. We have already cited Glyn's views on this point (see note 10 of chapter 2), and noted the general consensus that transnational production

makes life difficult for unions. It is perhaps worth observing, given our earlier asides on Ford's purposive development of an integrated theatre of European operations in the context of Britain's entry to the EEC, that observers of the great American car firm (see, for example, Cowling and Sugden 1987: 64–5, 74–7) have claimed an increasing flexing of industrial muscles in the 1970s and 1980s, in its dealings both with the British government and also with British trade unions (the instances given refer to the recurrence of threatened withdrawals of investment from the United Kingdom in the 1970s and 1980s).

2. When founded, the Ford Dagenham site was the 'Detroit of Europe' (Collins and Stratton 1993: 120), both because it was for a time the largest car factory in Europe and because when founded it incorporated on the Michigan pattern its own power station and steel works, as well as areas for components and assembly operations – the 'little River Rouge' (Reich 1990: 75). The Ford Halewood site, to which we briefly refer again below, was established in the 1960s.

3. The details of these other cases lie outside the scope of a single chapter; but interested readers will find a study of the Rover-BMW case in Coffey (2006: chapter 3), albeit from the viewpoint of controversy over the efficacy of 'Japanization' efforts in UK manufacturing.

4. Both the Cologne and Valencia sites being also already established plants: details of these sites and of Ford's European production networks can be found in Bonin et al. (2003).

5. A factory planner might of course envisage basic hourly or overtime rates increasing with the projected scale of plant activity, and factor this into a projected cost analysis, although if fixed costs are sufficiently large average costs of production overall would still be predicted to fall with an increase in the scale of activity (as per the illustrative scale curve). We can safely abstract from this kind of complication, because to do so is fully consistent with Ford's evidence.

6. The short technical addendum to this chapter expands upon what this entails. This device is nonessential from the viewpoint of our argument, but facilitates visual representation.

7. Other cost considerations might in some circumstances be an issue: for example, distance from suppliers (material transport costs) or customers (distribution costs). But neither these nor any other factors additional to those we assess in this chapter were mentioned in the course of the evidence given by Ford and the trade unions to the parliamentary committee.

8. See note 1 of this chapter, and note 10 of chapter 2.

9. For example, suppose a workforce is divided between two car lines at a single plant location, and there is believed in each case to be a 50 per cent chance of future hiring and a 50 per cent chance that workers will need to be let go, owing to fluctuations in the demand for cars. If the forecast employment swings are symmetric then there would be even odds that workers not needed on one car line could simply be moved across to the

other. But if the two production lines were housed at different locations and this option disappears, then the firm would definitely face hiring or firing costs at each plant location – thereby increasing its costs globally.

10. And which Ford has recently been in the process of selling again, a consequence of its mounting financial difficulties in the United States, even before the current financial crisis.

11. It is important to highlight this definite testimony, because when the trade unions later appeared before the parliamentary committee there was again much concern about the possible impact of 'short-term' thinking spurred by an undervalued euro (see HC 2000–2001:36). That Ford would be correct in taking a longer view on currency issues is amply borne out since. The reference given above for Tolliday (2003) is to a survey of Ford's history in the United Kingdom; insofar as this recent history is concerned, our assessment of the Dagenham closure differs somewhat.

12. We should perhaps note, since the Committee's report is a little blurred on this distinction, that that key point is not whether the closure of the Ford Dagenham site reduced the capacity ceiling of the company's investment structure measured against the output potentials of its complex of factory sites as a whole, since it is possible to change the physical capacities of a car assembly line without relocating it. The issue is not one of capacity ceilings in this sense. Capacity in this connection is relevant only because a reduction in forecast demand that increases the pressure of fixed costs can be signified by the emergence of overcapacity. In the expository diagrams employed we assume, for simplicity, that capacity ceilings are the same regardless of how many plant sites are selected across which to subdivide production, because in no sense did the Dagenham closure hinge on the physical capacity ceiling of a car assembly line.

13. A similar defence came from General Motors (Vauxhall) vis-à-vis developments at its British site in Luton, also under investigation by the Committee: while a similar response would apply here as for Ford, one wonders if corporate notes were compared before the exam.

14. Ford gave its oral evidence to the parliamentary committee on 24 May 2000. The seemingly contrary statement to the GLA cited in the final Committee report came later.

15. See *Guardian*, 29 March 2000 p. 26.

16. The Dagenham ward has become a high-profile 'success' for the British National Party, while the Ford Dagenham complex – including parts of its union structure – has long been the subject of comment as a place of activity for extreme elements on the political right.

17. Now called the Department of Business, Enterprise and Regulatory Reform.

18. We omit the break down into major categories (see www.autoindustry. co.uk), but what is generally evident is that the trend across all auto products is broadly similar. The DTI submission referred not just to car assembly, but to the larger sector, so this fact is also germane. The largest employment category is vehicles and engines, followed by auto parts; as

a share of UK manufacturing output, the sector's position as a whole was (broadly) stable.

19. The phrase 'lean production' was used in Womack et al. (1990) to describe a survey-based claim of worldwide resource productivity advantages in Japanese car assembly plants. Our view on this issue is that a careful reassessment of the original survey data upon which this claim was staked can be interpreted to show quite contrary things. As Coffey (2006: chapter 4; see also Coffey and Thornley 2006, 2008) observe, labour productivity was overestimated to the extent to which participating car plants worked with overtime, giving a likely bias towards Japanese sites; while in any case, and even before taking this into account, the data could more reasonably be interpreted as showing that while plants based in Europe and regardless of ownership performed differently on the suspect labour productivity measure, there was a distinct lack of evidence to suggest that Japanese plants (anywhere) enjoyed net advantages. We might contrast this position with that of other critics: for example, Williams et al. (1994), who tend rather to dismiss the original survey data collated by Womack et al. altogether.

20. This comment is informed by interviews carried out by one of the authors (Coffey) in 1999 with representatives of the Transport and General Workers Union: a fuller discussion of the issues here lies beyond the scope of this chapter, but is one subtext for workplace tensions. It is striking, however, that in this instance 'lean production' was invoked on the union side.

4   The Self-Effacing State: Private Services Required

1. This was the particular perspective of Mandel (1978: 488), for whom hypertrophy of the state (literally the opposite of atrophy) was an 'inevitable' and 'necessary' feature of mature capitalism: 'the rearguard action of declining capitalism...a generalized proclamation of the advantages of organization', replacing an earlier regard for 'competition' (ibid.: 500). For Mandel, the ideology of late capitalism was exemplified in the growing popularity of writers like J.K. Galbraith – vis-à-vis Galbraith's views on 'the new industrial state'.

2. Tony Benn's diaries for the period when he was briefly minister responsible for implementing a Labour Party commitment in the mid-1970s to extending public ownership across profitable as well as unprofitable sections of industry, give a good sense of the contrary pressures and heightened sensitivities of the time (see Benn 1989) (1973–1976).

3. Naomi Klein's (2007) thesis on the 'shock doctrine' gives equal weight both to the suddenness of the policy transformation in Britain, and its opportunistic features.

4. Thus the ensuing proliferation of variously appearing 'Offices of X Regulation': OFFER, OFGAS, OFRR, OFTEL, OFWAT. Florio (2004) provides a comprehensive review, with due attention to the

difficulties privatization brought for consumers and investment. Sawyer and O'Donnell (1999) offer criticism of the assumptions of 'regulated privatization'.

5. For a relatively recent overview and review of developments here, see ILO (2005).

6. Andrew Glyn, a severe critic of PFI, may understate the previous transforming potential of the scheme for this reason: 'this form of funding has contributed to 10 to 15 per cent of public services investment since 1997' (Glyn 2006: 43). David Coates' (2005c; see in particular ibid.: 68–69, 93, 118–124, 193) helpful discussion of the progress of PFI schemes – and of 'public private partnerships' more generally, as well as Gordon Browns' 'own bit of discrete privatization' elsewhere (see ibid.: 68) – uses indicative figures for the general size of the PFI scheme which seem consistent with gross rather than net magnitudes. We should note, however, that a second estimate for a later financial year (2005–2006) (the figure cited in the main text was estimated by Sawyer for 2001–2002) provides a lower estimate for the net investment share, falling below one fifth of public net investment as a whole (see Sawyer 2005: 240). The ordure into which the scheme has fallen – the Scottish National Party took control of the Scottish Parliament on pledges that included 'no more PFI' – may mean that this kind of falling off continues: nonetheless, earlier estimates may err on the side of parsimony.

7. See, for example, Sawyer (2003), and Pollock and Price (2004), both already cited; and for a detailed discussion of developments in the NHS, see Pollock (2005). George Monbiot's early investigate critique of *The Captive State* (see Monbiot 2001), also contains much indicative material. As an example of someone with forensically minded accounting skills investigating PFI, see the paper by Froud (2003). All of these works sit on the critical side – Giddens (2002), on the positive side, and briefly touched on below, is sanguine about these issues.

8. In our discussion we set aside issues raised by general price inflation: for PFI contracts the future income streams guaranteed by the state are typically set in real terms, with adjustments for future inflation contingent on actual inflation built in (see Sawyer 2003:174); accordingly, we can abstract, more or less safely, from this complication in our analysis. Thus both in our hypothesized thought experiment and in our broader assessment we ignore this issue.

9. The curve is negatively sloped and convex to the origin in the diagram, provided that at least one positive sum of money is paid in at least one future period.

10. The simple annuities formula for payments in perpetuity takes the annual payments and divides it by the real rate of return to obtain the 'current' value of the asset. In this example, for instance, if the real rate of return expected by consortium A were to rise to 15 per cent, then consortium B would now be willing to commit *three* times the resources today; the proportionate difference would be 200 per cent, and the

minimum efficiency difference (MED) curve would have three times the vertical height of the reference curve CC; etc.

11. This would be consistent with the post-World War II history of government borrowing to fund increases in public expenditure, although it is unlikely that the costs of capital for finance obtained by this route would have risen to anything like the costs on PFI schemes.

12. The Treasury's real rate of discount for comparisons of PFI expenditure streams and Public Sector Comparators is given at 6 per cent in the examples discussed in Sawyer (2003), which can be compared with the 2 ½ per cent real post-tax rate of return on government bonds, and the higher – and sometimes substantially higher – returns expected by consortia. A discussion of developments here is given in Sawyer (2005). See also Pollock and Price (2004).

13. The built-in cost overruns assumed for Public Sector Comparators (PSCs) in bidding processes for PFI contracts have confused several different issues in the literature: these cost overruns have generally been justified under the banner of 'risk transfer'. But this is merely part of the processes by which PFI contracts are determinedly sanctioned by the state: from the viewpoint of third-party financers, the premiums they claim for 'risk' will be reflected in the rates of interest they demand on the debts incurred by private sector consortia. It may be that by referring to 'built-in' risk Anthony Giddens is simply thinking of the Treasury process: but this process expressly elects to ignore questions of differential borrowing costs.

14. The acrimony here, and not least from parliamentary watchdogs, has been considerable, and steps have gradually been taken by the Treasury to prevent this. But in the same way that regulation of industries privatized by Mrs Thatcher in the 1980s were only regulated with a lag and after problems became evident (see note 4), this hints of a lack of preparation.

15. See, for example, Sawyer and O'Donnell's (1999: 19–30) survey of the British evidence, and also Florio (2004: especially ibid.: chapter 4).

16. See Florio (2004) for a thorough review of price and distribution effects.

17. As Sawyer (2003) also notes, the resulting arrangement over the long term is marked by a definite loss of flexibility vis-à-vis the use of assets: alternative uses of PFI projects are rendered impossible, without (costly) contract renegotiation.

5   The Self-Deceiving State: The 'Model Employer' Myth

1. A very comprehensive review of key global trends in liberalization, and of corporate interests (particularly US-based) in sponsoring it, is given in ILO (2006) (see also chapter 4 note 5).

2. See Cole (1969) and Gibb (2004: 288). Anyone visiting Owen's New Lanark complex becomes aware – as did Owen himself – of tensions between 'normative' and 'rational' objectives as these terms are explained below.

3. For example, one of India's oldest and largest business conglomerates, the giant Tata Group (comprising 98 companies operating in six continents, and including the automotive sector) lists its attributes in employee relations under family values, and cites the American writer Thoreau on morals. Its townships are held up as epitomes of communal existence, and its website notes the virtuous ways in which the rationalization of 100,000 jobs and a smooth transition of former public companies into Tata ownership have been achieved. It states it is striving to be a model employer. See www.tata.com (accessed 8 January 2008). Again, it demonstrates the variety of influences discussed below, ranging from cooperative, through normative, to rational.

4. Executive Order 26 February 1995.

5. In 'From Red Tape to Results: Creating a Government that Works Better and Costs Less', *National Performance Review*, 1994 p. 84, Diane Publishing.

6. See for example: 'New Freedom Initiative: A Progress Report', March 2004 by White House Domestic Policy Council, with respect to integrating Americans with disabilities into the workforce and promoting the federal government as a model employer of people with disabilities: http://www.whitehouse.gov/infocus/newfreedom/newfreedom-report-2004.pdf (accessed 8 January 2008).

7. See http://www.eeoc.gov/initiatives/lead/presentation_workforce.html (accessed 8 January 2008).

8. See, for example, Kessler and Purcell (1994); Farnham, Horton, and Giles (1994); Mailly, Dimmock, and Sethi (1989:115); Thomson (1983: 144); Bach and Winchester (1994: 263).

9. See, for example, Bach (1999) (see especially ibid.: 114), responding in part to the critique of theoretical analyses based on 'model employer' accounts raised by Thornley (1995) drawing on her work on nursing. Bach argued that nurses represented an 'exceptional' case – thereby asserting the account for the remaining groups.

10. See http://www.dh.gov.uk/en/Publicationsandstatistics/Publications/PublicationsPolicyAndGuidance/Browsable/DH 5675761 (accessed 8 January 2008).

11. This is in no way to diminish the importance of exploring each of these features, and in tandem – see, for example, Thornley (1996, 2001) for the health services in the United Kingdom, and Thornley (2004, 2007b) for local government.

12. Lower bound estimates start at around two thirds of total employment, depending on source.

13. While a quarter of all work in the whole economy is part-time, the percentage rises considerably if looking only at women (44%) (see Thornley 2006). For a good discussion of gendered temporary work in the public services, see Conley (2003).

14. For source and a fuller discussion of these measures see Thornley (2006). While the current figures for the internal public sector gap for 2007 stands at 21 per cent (see next chapter) this is calculated from a discontinuous series as NES was replaced in 2004 by ASHE.

15. The 'internal' gender pay gap within local government is wider than the public sector aggregate gap, and the gap between NJC female workers measured against all-economy men actually widened between 1998 and 2002 – under the watch of New Labour – and is higher than the economy-wide gender pay gap.
16. The study in Thornley (1998) finds deterioration between 1979 and 1998 against comparator groups.
17. For an outstanding study of the impact of low pay on the working poor, see Toynbee (2003).
18. Coates (2005c: 82) on this point notes the 'massive reluctance' with which New Labour responded to EU Directives on labour law.
19. Particularly the Single Status Agreements in local government, and Agenda for Change in health.
20. Equalities Act 2006. For a discussion of this, and a detailed analysis of equalities initiatives in the NHS, see Thornley 2007a, 2008. A new Equalities Bill is currently also under discussion.
21. See, for example, Thornley 2008.
22. Coates (2005c: 190–5, 213) notes that the budgetary constraints facing New Labour, if unwilling to raise taxes and where economic growth alone is insufficient, results in the de facto exploitation of public sector workers.

6   New Ways or the Abject State

1. The ditching of the clause, which committed the party (in principle) to policies of 'common ownership' was symbolic in the sense of the assurances given to the private sector that New Labour would not return to nationalization, as noted in Chapter 4, and was a party for business. This aspect has been widely discussed: 'Blair argued that the new Clause 4 made Labour a party of "aspiration and ambition" ' (Driver and Martell 1998: 26). It also had elements of a contrived 'showdown' with recalcitrant supporters: the defenestration was resisted by some unions but ultimately ushered through on the back of a referendum of constituency members seeking approval of the newly worded resolution without allowing a direct vote on which was preferred.
2. The 'prudence' claimed by Gordon Brown was oddly enough assented to by the City even after PFI-debts steadily accumulated and private consumption and mortgage debts mounted.
3. In his engaging 'sociological' critique Prideaux (2005) makes a good fist of demolishing New Labour's intellectual pretensions vis-à-vis the communitarian strands in its social policy. But while accepting the value of this line of inquiry – see also Bevir (2005) – and of the kinds of critical analyses which emerge, the authoritarian premises that many identify in parts of New Labour policy formulation and rhetoric in questions of 'rights and responsibilities' sit easily with other well-trodden traditions, consonant with British Conservatism. Thus at about the same time that

'communitariansim' was being conjured on the left and centre, more conservative tracts were circulating from the right, with one Institute of Economic Affairs book making much of the sound effect on formative character of the harsher judicial developments of the early nineteenth century vis-à-vis the 'poor' – a 'mischievously ambiguous' term (Himmelfarb 1995: 125) – and calling for a similar distinction to be made today between the 'deserving' and the 'undeserving'.

4. Pluralism does not, of course, imply consensus: disagreements and conflicts are recognized, but generally viewed as susceptible to solution. However, some of the less 'interventionist' contributions to the stakeholding debate are more unitarist in their construction of philosophies of corporate governance: see Driver and Martell (1998: 52–53) on Kay (1993), supporting legislative institutionalization of an expanded range of corporate responsibilities and a 'trustee' model of ownership, but chary of any dilution of managerial authority over employees.

5. Giddens has himself quickly tired of the 'third way' phrase – see Giddens (2002) – while sticking more or less consistently to the basic thrust of his views therein.

6. For example, Giddens (2000) responds to selected criticisms; the collections in Hutton and Giddens (2001), or Giddens and Diamond (2005), include some emphatic restatements of core tenets, as well as some less direct responses to critics; or one can visit Giddens' recent advice to Gordon Brown, on the importance of keeping up with New Labour (Giddens 2007).

7. We have already touched upon objections to the Fordism/post-Fordism dichotomy in Chapter 2, and will return to this point again in the concluding chapter of this book.

8. We have again already touched on these points at various junctures in this book.

9. See also Coates and Hay (2001), which is likewise valuable in this regard.

10. On the twin themes of 'economic dynamism' and 'social cohesion', an affinity with similar couplings in the United States at this time has again been noted. 'All of this bears comparison', Driver and Martell (1998) note, 'with the policies of the US Democrats and the approach of US politicians such as Robert Reich, former secretary of state for labour under Clinton' (ibid.: 57). The quotation Coates makes here is from Tony Blair's speech to the European Socialists Congress, in Malmo Sweden, undertaken on 6 June 1997 (see Coates 2005c: 222 note 30).

11. Care must be taken not to accept propaganda at its own face value and assume that previous governments were not, as a rule, 'interested' in education, skills, or technical know-how. The massive shortfall in skills for 'core' workers generally noted in Britain before 1997 – for examples and references see Coates (2005c: 10; also ibid. 217 note 30) – is not readily separated from the de-industrialization of the British economy in earlier decades, a point also emphasized by commentators like Kitson and Michie (1996) for investment questions more generally.

12. While both the claimant count and Labour Force Survey (LFS) measures of unemployment (see note 3 Chapter 2) showed some reductions over the period as a whole, there was widespread scepticism as to the existence of 'hidden unemployment' in the form of workers registered as disabled and so not included in the claimant count and 'inactive' vis-à-vis the LFS survey. For a discussion also of persistent job deficits in some areas, see Theodore (2007).

13. A good all-round discussion of poverty in Britain for the period encompassing the time-frame of Coates survey, as well as historical context, can be found in Alcock (2006).

14. Kitson and Wilkinson (2007: 805) rightly draw attention to the role played by 'high levels of demand', and not least 'consumption expenditure', in driving UK economic growth; but, we should also be aware of the point, emphasized by Edmonds and Glyn (2005), and as cited in Coutts et al. (2007: 860), that public spending has played a very large role in net job creation.

15. Much of the inward foreign direct investment, in any case lagging behind outward, was directed in the period under review by Coates towards merger with or acquisitions of existing operations in the United Kingdom, rather than investment in net increments to capital stock. And problems are noted as continuing with regard both to spending on research and development and to the productivity gap with OECD countries (see Coates 2005c: 174–178). A tendency also noted by Coates for New Labour to exhort on improved business practices with little success is consistent with the anomalies very much in evidence in the DTI evidence to the Trade and Industry Committee vis-à-vis the 'lean revolution', touched upon in Chapter 3.

16. This is also consistent with concerns expressed, for example, in Oughton's (2003) overview of evolving concepts of 'competitiveness' vis-à-vis industrial policy in the years before and after the first New Labour government, which like Wilkinson's (2007) comprehensive assessment of key UK economic trends notes that such productivity gains as enjoyed by UK-based manufacturing sites over the past several decades have been achieved largely by employment 'downsizing' rather than output expansion, for sale at home or abroad. We should be mindful, of course, that this partly reflects the production sourcing decisions of transnational firms.

17. Furthermore, the tax concessions to lower income families introduced to supplement the minimum wage were knocked out again after the period surveyed in Coates (2005c), almost as an administrative oversight, occasioning a political crisis for Prime Minister Gordon Brown. In 1999, a lower tax band of 10 per cent had been introduced to help low-income families, but in his last budget as Chancellor of the Exchequer Brown abolished this while reducing the basic rate of tax from 22 to 20 per cent, helping the better off at the expense of the poorest. Concessions followed later as the effects became obvious, but without complete compensation.

18. Authors' calculations from Annual Survey of Hours and Earnings (Ashe), 2008. The gender pay gap for the same year within the public sector for full-time workers is circa 21 per cent.
19. A lifetime gap of circa £369,000 has been identified (Equality and Human Rights Commission), and the United Kingdom currently stands at 81st out of 130 in the World Economic Forum Global Gender Gap Index on 'wage equality' measures (*Guardian* 14 November 2008). Estimates for equalization currently vary between 2195 (Chartered Management Institute cited in Times 19 September 2008, for women managers) to 2085 (Equality Bill June 2008: 7).
20. See, for example, the extended discussion in Brenner (2005).
21. Gallie also contrasts the employment regimes approach with two other major approaches: *universalistic theories,* like Braverman's (1974) thesis on the universal tendencies within capitalism towards 'deskilling' for the mass of workers, and *theories of production regimes* – in which category he includes the Hall-Soskice VoC framework, discussed above.

7 The End of Things: The Great Financial Crisis

1. See in particular Brummer's (2008) study *The Crunch: The Scandal of Northern Rock and the Escalating Credit Crisis,* written from the perspective of a financial journalist and very critical of the behaviour of the Northern Rock board, the Bank of England governor, the Chancellor of the Exchequer, the Financial Services Authority (FSA), and the bonus culture in financial trading (see also his follow up: Brummer 2009).
2. An evident unwillingness on the part of banks to pass these interest rate cuts on to customers has added to the opprobrium currently being heaped on the financial sector.
3. We have previously described in Chapter 6, and in connection with Coates' (2005c) audit of New Labour and other commentaries, some of which are also touched on by Elliot and Atkinson, the inability of the UK-based manufacturing sector to satisfy the consumer boom.
4. See *Guardian* 28 January 2009.
5. In response to a question on why a multi-billion-pound banks bailout had failed to filter through to taxpaying bank users, the words 'saved the world' came out, before Gordon Brown corrected himself to clarify 'we not only worked with other countries to save the world's banking system ...' (see *Times* 10 December 2008).
6. Sustained public protests have already taken place in Greece, Iceland, and France, and currently refinery strikes in the United Kingdom indicate growing disquiet over employment. Concerns are now being expressed about the Eurozone countries, especially the capacity of richer countries to maintain 'Continental social democracy' within both the constraints of EU rules and in the face of growing pressures to bail out poorer countries. There are also concerns about investments in the Baltic region.

7. Pension fund organizations are the latest to press for more government help. It has been reported that a quarter of major private sector firms expect to close their final salary pension schemes to *existing* members in the next few years (BBC News 23 January 2009).
8. One of Obama's first moves has been to propose, with Congress leaders, the wide-ranging American Recovery and Reinvestment Act, which involves some $275 billion in economic recovery tax cuts and $550 billion in investments. This is aimed at rescuing the US economy, creating millions of jobs and 'greening' the country's infrastructure, and covers investment in alternative energy and construction projects. It also includes an expansion of healthcare coverage, student grants, unemployment and food stamp benefits, and is aimed at protecting public services and jobs. It has been widely reported as a clear echo of Franklin Roosevelt's New Deal (*Observer* 25 January 2009). Somewhat reminiscent of the early period in the Clinton administration, the AFL-CIO have reported that some members of Congress are already seeking to stop this critical legislation – and Republican party criticism is starting to grow.

8　Strange Days

1. For example, there is a debate concerning the relative weight attaching to wage-effort bargaining advantages in the investment-location decisions of transnational producers and the role of other factors relevant to strategic decision making, including product market uncertainty: see Cowling and Sugden (1998), and the comment by Dunn (2001). The Ford case is one in which the ability to hedge against uncertain product markets uncertain product markets by means of consolidating production at a reduced number of sites seems to be contingently sacrificed for reasons likely to have included bargaining advantages over workers. The case thus contributes to this literature (see also Coffey and Tomlinson 2006; and Chapter 2 note 10).
2. We have already observed in the relevant chapter that the most comprehensive survey of the effects of privatization in Britain provides little support for this kind of assertion. The same could be said for mainstream economic theory, increasingly critical of this kind of mantra. A good introduction to some relevant issues, from a 'principal-agent' perspective is provided by the economist Johan Willner (1999), amongst Europe's most able practitioners, who in a formal review develops some of the implications of recent work by other theorists, including demonstrations that (a) increased external competition can in some instances induce more rather than less 'managerial slack' within organizations, and (b) organizations which rely on the appeal of the job as a means of motivating employees may find management based on administered rewards and punishments 'counterproductive', because crowding out 'intrinsic' motivation. A later paper – Willner (2003) – offers a suitably probing review of privatization.

3. We might note that in the 1980s much space was given to post-Fordist themes as a means of explaining the economic and social dislocations of Thatcherism, and its electoral success, usually with reference to the influence of writers like Stuart Hall as well as the example set by *Marxism Today*, magazine publication of the British Communist Party as was. Subsequently, analogies have been suggested with the shift from 'old' to New Labour: see, for example, Driver and Martell (1998: 42–43), Dworkin (2007: 72–73), or Gilbert (2008: 44–46) (the last two of which bear interesting comparison with Buechler (2000), cited in note 14 of Chapter 2). It is perhaps also worth noting that post-Fordist themes segue easily into the proposition that modern capitalist economies are somehow 'post-industrial', and that old economy sectors like manufacturing are no longer economically important, ignoring both the tradability of manufactures compared to services and the empirical evidence on backward and forward linkages between manufacture and other sectors. As Elliot and Atkinson (2008: 178–183) observe in connection with the 'myth' of the 'creative' or 'knowledge-based economy', this makes for bad policy, although the idea is also one that meshes easily with New Labour rhetoric on a 'meritocracy' of skills.

4. We have previously touched on the 'othering' of Japan in connection with debates about comparative production practices, a relevant issue when considering some of the many uses made of the idea of lean production in the literature on alleged innovations in Western manufacturing practices (see the references given in Chapter 3 note 19; also Coffey and Thornley (2007; 2008); and Pulignano et al. (2008)). Coates (2007) provides a first-rate review of changing Western perceptions on Japan as the comparative fortunes of its national economy have waxed and waned over the post-Second World War period; see Bailey et al. (2007) more generally.

5. See Coffey (2009) for a succinct overview of the life history of British Leyland.

6. We will side step, in this book, a discussion of agency versus structure, one of the more intractable problems of social and historical research. 'Opportunism', however, which may manifest itself in both rational and irrational ways, implies both agency and contingency.

7. The issue of migrant labour, as of gender, is a major area waiting systematic exploration within the varieties of capitalism literature, as it is now rapidly developing.

References

Abrahamson, E. (1997) 'The Emergence and Prevalence of Employee Management Rhetorics: The Effects of Long Waves, Labor Unions, and Turnover, 1875–1992', *Academy of Management Journal*, 40: 491–533.

Addison, J.T., Heywood, J.S., and Wei, X. (2003) 'New Evidence on Unions and Plant Closings: Britain in the 1990s', *Southern Economic Journal*, Vol. 69, No. 4: 822–841.

Alcock, P. (2006) *Understanding Poverty*, 3rd Edition, Houndmills, Basingstoke, and New York: Palgrave MacMillan.

Allen, V. (1960) *Trade Unions and the Government*, London: Longmans.

Angeriz, A. and Chakravarty, S.P. (2007) 'Changing Patterns of UK poverty, 1997–2004', *Cambridge Journal of Economics*, Vol. 31, No. 6, November: 995–1006.

Bach, S. (1999) 'NHS Pay Bargaining Reform and the Consequences of Local Pay: From Whitley to the Market', *Historical Studies in Industrial Relations*, 8(Autumn): 99–115.

Bach, S. and Winchester, D. (1994) 'Opting Out of Pay Devolution? The Prospects for Local Pay Bargaining in UK Public Services', *British Journal of Industrial Relations*, Vol. 32, No. 2: 263–282.

Bach, S. and Winchester, D. (2003) 'Industrial Relations in the Public Sector', in P. Edwards (ed.) *Industrial Relations: Theory and Practice* (2nd Edition). Oxford: Blackwell, 285–312.

Bailey, D., Coffey, D., and Tomlinson, P.R. (eds) (2007) *Crisis or Recovery in Japan: State and Industrial Economy*, Cheltenham and Northampton, MA: Edward Elgar.

Barley, S.R. and Kunda, G. (1992) 'Design and Devotion: Surges of Rational and Normative Ideologies of Control in Managerial Discourses', *Administrative Science Quarterly*, Vol. 37: 363–399.

Bayliss, F. (1962) *British Wages Councils*, Oxford: Blackwell.

Beaumont, P.B. (1992) *Public Sector Industrial Relations*, London and New York: Routledge.

Benn, T. (1987) *Out of the Wilderness: Diaries 1963–67*, London: Arrow Books Ltd.

Benn, T. (1989) *Against the Tide: Diaries 1973–76*, London: Arrow Books Ltd.

Bercusson, B. (1978) *Fair Wages Resolutions*, London: Mansell.

Best, M. H. (1990) *The New Competition: Institutions of Industrial Restructuring*, Cambridge, UK: Polity Press.

Bevir, M. (2005) *New Labour: A Critique*, London and New York: Routledge.

Bhaskar, K. (1979) *The Future of the UK Motor Industry*, London: Poland Street Publications Ltd.

Bonin, H., Lung, Y., and Tolliday, S. (eds) (2003) *Ford: The European History 1903–2003, Volume 1 and Volume 2*, Paris: Editions P.L.A.G.E.

Bowring, F. (1997) 'Communitarianism and Morality: In Search of the Subject', *New Left Review*, 222: 93–113.

Braverman, H. (1974) *Labor and Monopoly Capital: The Degradation of Work in the Twentieth Century*, New York and London: Monthly Review Press.

Brenner, R. (2005) 'The Capitalist Economy, 1945–2000: A Reply to Konings and to Panitch and Gindin', in D. Coates (ed.) *Varieties of Capitalism, Varieties of Approaches*, Houndmills, Basingstoke, and New York: Palgrave MacMillan, 211–241.

Brummer, A. (2008) *The Crunch: The Scandal of Northern Rock and the Escalating Credit Crisis*, London: Random House.

Brummer, A. (2009) *The Crunch: How Greed and Incompetence Sparked the Credit Crisis*, London: Random House.

Buechler, S.M. (2000) *Social Movements in Advanced Capitalism: The Political Economy and Cultural Construction of Social Activism*, Oxford and New York: Oxford University Press.

Carter, B. and Fairbrother, P. (1999) 'The Transformation of British Public Sector Industrial Relations from "Model Employer" to Marketised Relations', *Historical Studies in Industrial Relations*, 7(Spring): 119–146.

Clay, H. (1929) *The Problem of Industrial Relations*, London: Macmillan.

Clegg, H.A. (1967) 'Employers', in H.A. Clegg and A. Flanders (eds) *The System of Industrial Relations in Great Britain*, Oxford: Blackwell.

Clegg, H. and Chester, T. (1957) *Wage Policy and the Health Service*, Oxford: Basil Blackwell.

Coates, D. (2000) *Models of Capitalism: Growth and Stagnation in the Modern Era*, Cambridge: Polity Press.

Coates, D. (2005a) 'Choosing between Paradigms – A Personal View', in D. Coates (ed.) *Varieties of Capitalism, Varieties of Approaches*, Houndmills, Basingstoke, and New York: Palgrave MacMillan, 265–271.

Coates, D. (2005b) 'Paradigms of Explanation', in D. Coates (ed.) *Varieties of Capitalism, Varieties of Approaches*, Houndmills, Basingstoke, and New York: Palgrave MacMillan, 1–25.

Coates, D. (2005c) *Prolonged Labour: The Slow Birth of New Labour Britain*, Houndmills, Basingstoke, and New York: Palgrave MacMillan.

Coates, D. (2007) 'The Rise and Fall of Japan as a Model of "Progressive Capitalism"', in D. Bailey, D. Coffey, and P.R. Tomlinson (eds) *Crisis or Recovery in Japan: State and Industrial Economy Japan*, Cheltenham and Northampton MA: Edward Elgar, 179–196.

Coates, D. and Hay, C. (2001) 'The Internal and External Face of New Labour's Political Economy', *Government and Opposition*, Vol. 36, No. 4: 442–471.

Coffey, D. (2006) *The Myth of Japanese Efficiency: The World Car Industry in a Globalizing Age*, Cheltenham and Northampton, MA: Edward Elgar.

Coffey, D. (2009) 'Production Counterfeits and Policy Collisions: The Rover Trajectory – A Salutary Tale', in M. Freyssenet (ed.) *The New Automobile World in the 21st Century*, Basingstoke and New York: Palgrave MacMillan.

Coffey, D. and Thornley, C. (2006) 'Automotive Assembly: Automation, Motivation and Lean Production Reconsidered', *Assembly Automation: The*

International Journal of Assembly Technology and Management, Vol. 26, No. 2: 98–103.

Coffey, D. and Thornley, C. (2007) ' "Can Japan Compete": Reconsidered', in D. Bailey, D. Coffey, and P.R. Tomlinson (eds) *Crisis or Recovery in Japan: State and Industrial Economy*, Cheltenham and Northampton, MA: Edward Elgar, 197–215.

Coffey, D. and Thornley, C. (2008) 'Lean Production: The Original Myth Reconsidered', in V. Pulignano, P. Stewart, A. Danford, and A.M. Richardson (eds) *Flexibility at Work: Developments in the International Automobile Industry*, Basingstoke and New York: Palgrave MacMillan, 83–103.

Coffey, D. and Tomlinson, P.R. (2003) 'Globalisation, Vertical Relations and the J-mode Firm', *Journal of Post Keynesian Economics*, Vol. 26, No. 1, Fall: 117–144.

Coffey, D. and Tomlinson, P.R. (2006) 'Multiple Facilities, Strategic Splitting and Vertical Structures: Stability, Growth and Distribution Reconsidered', *The Manchester School*, Vol. 74, No. 5, September: 558–576.

Cole, N. (1969) *Robert Owen of New Lanark 1771–1858*, New York: Augustus M. Kelley.

Collins, P. and Stratton, M. (1993) *British Car Factories from 1896: A Complete Historical, Geographical, Architectural & Technological Survey*, Dorset: Veloce Publishing Plc.

Conley, H. (2003) 'Temporary Work in the Public Services: Implications for Equal Opportunities', *Gender, Work and Organisation*, Vol. 10, No. 4: 455–477.

Coutts, K., Glyn, A., and Rowthorn, B. (2007) 'Structural Change under New Labour', *Cambridge Journal of Economics*, Vol. 31, No. 6, November: 845–861.

Cowling, K. (1982) *Monopoly Capitalism*, London and Basingstoke: The MacMillan Press Ltd.

Cowling, K. (1986) 'The Internationalization of Production and De-industrialization', in A. Amin and J. Goddard (eds) *Technological Change, Industrial Restructuring and Regional Development*, London: Allen & Unwin, 23–40.

Cowling, K. and Sugden, R. (1987) *Transnational Monopoly Capitalism*, Sussex: Wheatsheaf Book and New York: St. Martin's Press.

Cowling, K. and Sugden, R. (1998) 'The Essence of the Modern Corporation: Markets, Strategic Decision-making and the Theory of the Firm', *The Manchester School*, Vol. 66, No. 1: 59–86.

Driver, S. and Martell, L. (1998) *New Labour: Politics after Thatcherism*, Oxford and Malden MA: Polity Press.

Dunn, S.P. (2001) 'Uncertainty, Strategic Decision-Making and the Essence of the Modern Corporation: Extending Cowling and Sugden', *The Manchester School*, Vol. 69, No, 1: 31–41.

Dworkin, D. (2007) *Class Struggles*, Harlow: Pearson Education Limited.

Edmonds, J. and Glyn, A. (2005) 'Public Spending Alone Explains Britain's Jobs Growth', *Financial Times* 30 June.

Edwards, P., Hall, M., Hyman, R., Marginson, P., Sisson, K., Waddington, J., and Winchester, D. (1998) 'Great Britain: From Partial Collectivism to Neo-Liberalism to Where?' in A. Ferner and R. Hyman (eds) *Changing Industrial Relations in Europe*, Oxford: Blackwell.

Elliott, L. and Atkinson, D. (2007) *Fantasy Island*, London: Constable & Robinson.

Elliott, L. and Atkinson, D. (2008) *The Gods that Failed: How Blind Faith in Markets Has Cost Us Our Future*, London: Random House.

Farnham, D. and Pimlott, J. (1995) *Understanding Industrial Relations*, London: Cassell.

Farnham, D., Horton, S. and Giles, L. (1994) 'Human Resources Management and Industrial Relations in the Public Sector: From Model Employer to a Hybrid Model,' Paper to Employment Research Unit Annual Conference, Cardiff.

Fielden, S. and Whiting, F. (2006) 'The Psychological Contract: Is the UK National Health Service a Model Employer?' *Health Services Management Research*, Vol. 20, No. 2: 94–104.

Florio, M. (2004) *The Great Divestiture: Evaluating the Welfare Impact of the British Privatizations 1979–1997*, Cambridge, MA and London: The MIT Press.

Ford Blue Book (1997) *Agreements and Conditions of Employment: Hourly Paid Employees, Ford Motor Company Ltd* (company agreement).

Fredman, S. and Morris, G. (1989a) *The State as Employer: Labour Law in the Public Services*, London: Mansell

Fredman, S. and Morris, G. (1989b) 'The State as Employer: Setting a New Example', *Personnel Management*, August: 25–29.

Froud, J. (2003) 'The Private Finance Initiative: Risk, Uncertainty and the State', *Accounting, Organizations & Society*, Vol. 28, No.6: 567–589.

Gaffney, D., Pollock, A.M., Price, D., and Shaoul, J. (1999) 'PFI in the NHS – Is There an Economic Case', *British Medical Journal*, 319: 116–119.

Galbraith, James K. (2005) 'Galbraith: A Partisan Appraisal', in B. Laperche and D. Uzundis (eds) *John Kenneth Galbraith and the Future of Economics*, Houndsmills, Basingstoke, and New York: Palgrave MacMillan.

Gallie, D. (2007a) 'Production Regimes, Employment Regimes and the Quality of Work', in Gallie, D. (ed.) *Employment Regimes and the Quality of Work*, Oxford: Oxford University Press, 1–33.

Gallie, D. (2007b) 'The Quality of Work Life in Comparative Perspective', in Gallie, D. (ed.) *Employment Regimes and the Quality of Work*, Oxford: Oxford University Press, 205–232.

Gibb, S. (2004) 'Contemporary Analyses of the Model Employer: Is There a New Ideal?' *International Journal of Human Resources Development and Management*, Vol. 4, No. 3: 288–296.

Giddens, A. (1998) *The Third Way*, Cambridge, UK: Polity Press.

Giddens, A. (2000) *The Third Way and Its Critics*, Cambridge, UK: Polity Press.

Giddens, A. (2001) *Sociology*, 4th Edition, Cambridge, UK: Polity Press.

Giddens, A. (2002) *Where Now for New Labour?* Cambridge, UK: Polity Press.

Giddens, A. (2007) *Over To You, Mr. Brown*, Cambridge, UK: Polity Press.

Giddens, A. and Diamond, P. (eds) (2005) *The New Egalitarianism*, Cambridge, UK: Polity Press.

Giddens, A. and Hutton, W. (2001a) 'In Conversation', in W. Hutton and A. Giddens (eds) *On the Edge: Living with Global Capitalism*, London: Vintage, 1–51.

Giddens, A. and Hutton, W. (2001b) 'Fighting Back', in W. Hutton and A. Giddens (eds) On the Edge: Living with Global Capitalism, London: Vintage, 213–214.

Gilbert, J. (2008) *Anticapitalism and Culture: Radical Theory and Popular Politics*, Oxford and New York: Berg.

Glyn, A. (2006) *Capitalism Unleashed: Finance, Globalization and Welfare*, Oxford: Oxford University Press.

Glyn, A. and Sutcliffe, B. (1972) *British Capitalism, Workers and the Profits Squeeze*, Harmondsworth: Penguin Books.

Griffiths, A. and Wall, S. (2007) *Applied Economics*, 11th Edition, Harlow: Pearson Education.

Hall, P.A. and Soskice, D. (2001) 'An Introduction to Varieties of Capitalism', in P.A. Hall and D. Soskice (eds) *Varieties of Capitalism: The Institutional Foundations of Comparative Advantage*, Oxford: Oxford University Press, 1–68.

Hall, P.A. (2007) 'The Evolution of Varieties of Capitalism in Europe', in B. Hancké, B., Rhodes, and Thatcher, M. (eds) *Beyond Varieties of Capitalism: Conflict, Contradictions and Complementarities in the European Economy*, Oxford: Oxford University Press, 39–85.

Hancké, B., Rhodes, M., and Thatcher, M. (2007) 'Introduction: Beyond Varieties of Capitalism', in B. Hancké, M. Rhodes, and M. Thatcher (eds) *Beyond Varieties of Capitalism: Conflict, Contradictions, and Complementarities in the European Economy*, Oxford: Oxford University Press, 3–38.

Harcourt, G. (2006) 'Paul Samuelson on Karl Marx: Were the Sacrificed Games of Tennis Worth It?' in M. Szenburg, L. Ramrattan, and A.A. Gottesman (eds) *Samuelsonian Economics and the Twenty First Century*, Oxford and New York: Oxford University Press, 127–141.

Harvey, J. and Hood, K. (1958) *The British State*, London: Lawrence & Wishart.

Hatzius, J. (2000) 'Foreign Direct Investment and Factor Demand Elasticities', *European Economic Review*, Vol. 44: 117–143.

Hay, C. (2005) 'Two Can Play at That Game…or Can They? Varieties of Capitalism, Varieties of Institutionalism', in D. Coates (ed.) *Varieties of Capitalism, Varieties of Approaches*, Houndmills, Basingstoke, and New York: Palgrave MacMillan, 106–121.

Haydu, J. and Lee, C. (2004) 'Model Employers and Good Government in the Late 19th and Late 20th Centuries', *Sociological Forum*, Vol. 19, No. 2: 177–202.

HC (2000–2001) *Vehicle Manufacturing in the UK: Report, Together with the Proceedings of the Committee, Minutes of Evidence, and Appendices*, House of Commons, Session 2000–01, Trade and Industry Committee (Third Report).

Hill, C. (2002) *The Century of Revolution: 1602–1714*, Second Edition, London and New York: Routledge Classics.

Himmelfarb, G. (1995) *The De-moralization of Society: From Victorian Values to Modern Values*, London: IEA Health and Welfare Unit.

Howes, C. and Singh, A. (2000) 'Introduction: Competitiveness Matters', in C. Howes and A. Singh (eds) *Competitiveness Matters: Industry and Economic Performance in the U.S.*, Ann Arbor: The University of Michigan Press, 1–28.

Huizinga, H. (1990) 'Unions, Taxes and the Structure of Multinational Enterprises', *Economics Letters*, Vol. 34: 73–75.

Hutton, W. (1995) *The State We're In*, London: Vintage.

Hutton, W. (2009) 'Unless We Are Decisive Britain Faces Bankruptcy', *Observer*, 18 January.

Hutton, W. and Giddens, A. (eds) (2001) *On the Edge: Living with Global Capitalism*, London: Vintage.

Hyman, R. (1989) *The Political Economy of Industrial Relations: Theory and Practice in a Cold Climate*, Basingstoke: Macmillan Press Ltd.

ILO (International Labour Organization) (2005/6) *Winners or Losers? Liberalizing Public Services*, edited by E. Rosskam, Geneva: International Labour Office.

Kaldor, N. (1978) 'The Effects of Devaluation on Trade in Manufactures', in N. Kaldor, (ed.) *Further Essays on Applied Economics*, London: Duckworth.

Kay, J. (1993) *The Foundations of Corporate Success*, Oxford: Oxford University Press.

Kessler, I. and Purcell, J. (1994) 'Strategic Choice and New Forms of Employment Relations in the Public Service Sector: Developing an Analytical Framework', Paper presented to Employment Research Unit Annual Conference, Cardiff Business School.

Kingsmill, D. (2001) The Kingsmill Review, http://www.kingsmillreview.gov.uk (accessed 9 November 2005).

Kitson, M. and Michie, J. (1996) 'Britain's Industrial Performance since 1960: Underinvestment and Relative Decline', *Economic Journal*, Vol. 106, No. 434 (January): 196–212.

Kitson, M. and Wilkinson, F. (2007) 'The Economics of New Labour Policy and Performance', *Cambridge Journal of Economics*, Vol. 31, No. 6, November: 805–816.

Klein, N. (2007) *The Shock Doctrine: The Rise of Disaster Capitalism*, London: Penguin Books (Allen Lane)

Krugman, P. (1994) 'Competitiveness: A Dangerous Obsession', *Foreign Affairs*, March–April: 28–44.

Labour Market Trends (2004) *Labour Market Trends*, July http://www.statistics.gov.uk, (accessed 12 March 2006).

Labour Market Trends (2006) *Public Sector Employment 2006: Seasonally Adjusted Series and Recent Trends*, Vol. 114, No. 12: 419–438.

Lash, S. and Urry, J. (1994) *Economies of Signs and Space*, London: SAGE Publications Ltd.

Livingstone, K. (2007) 'Davos 07: Why Should a Socialist Mayor Come?' http://commentisfree.guardian.co.uk/2007/01/davos_07_why_should_a_socialist_mayor-come, January 25, 10.00am (accessed 13.06.2007).

Local Government Pay Commission (LGPC) (2003), *Report of the Local Government Pay Commission* (kindly provided by UNISON).

Luria, D. (2000) 'A High Road Policy for U.S. Manufacturing', in C. Howes and A. Singh (eds) *Competitiveness Matters: Industry and Economic Performance in the U.S.*, Ann Arbor: The University of Michigan Press, 165–179.

Lyddon, D. (1996) 'The Myth of Mass Production and the Mass Production of Myth', *Historical Studies in Industrial Relations*, No. 1, March: 77–105.

Mailly, R., Dimmock, S., and Sethi, A. (eds) (1989), *Industrial Relations in the Public Services*, London: Routledge.

Mandel, E. (1978) *Late Capitalism*, London and New York: Verso.

Mann, C. (2000) 'Improving U.S. International Competitiveness: Macro-Policy Management vs. Managed Trade Policy', in C. Howes and A. Singh (eds) *Competitiveness Matters: Industry and Economic Performance in the U.S.*, Ann Arbor: The University of Michigan Press, 68–86.

McCarthy, W.E.J. and Clifford, B.A. (1966) 'The Works of Industrial Courts of Inquiry', *British Journal of Industrial Relations*, Vol. IV, No. 1.

Monbiot, G. (2001) *Captive State*, London: Pan.

Morgan, P. and Allington, N. (2002) 'Has the Public Sector Retained Its "Model Employer" Status?', *Public Money and Management*, January-March, 35–41.

National Performance Review (1994) *From Red Tape to Results: Creating a Government that Works Better and Costs Less*, Darby, DA: Diane Publishing.

Ngai-Ling, S. (2000) 'Globalization and Its 'Other(s): Three "New Kinds of Orientalism" and the Political Economy of Trans-Border Identity', in C. Hay and D. Marsh (eds) *Demystifying Globalization*, Basingstoke: MacMillan Press Ltd., 105–126.

Osler, D. (2002) *Labour Party PLC – New Labour as a Party of Business*, Edinburgh: Mainstream.

Oughton, C. (2003) 'Industrial Policy and Economic Development', in D. Coffey and C. Thornley (eds) *Industrial and Labour Market Policy and Performance: Issues and Perspectives*, London and New York: Routledge, 9–28.

Palmer, G., MacInnes, T., and Kenway, P. (2006) *Monitoring Poverty and Social Exclusion 2006*, York: Joseph Rowntree Foundation .

Pelling, H. (1968) *Popular Politics and Society in Late Victorian Britain*, London: Macmillan.

Peoples, J. and Sugden, R. (2000) 'Divide and Rule by Transnational Corporations', in C.N. Pitelis and R. Sugden (eds), *The Nature of the Transnational Firm*, London and New York: Routledge.

Phelps Brown, H. (1959) *The Growth of British Industrial Relations*, London: Macmillan.

Piore, M.J. and Sabel, C.F. (1984) *The Second Industrial Divide: Policies for Prosperity*, New York: Basic Books.

Pollock, A.M. and Price, D. (2004) *Public Risk for Private Gain*, London: UNISON.

Pollock, A.M., Leys, C., Price, D., Rowland, D., and Gnani, S. (2005) *NHS PLC: The Privatisation of Our Health Care*, London and New York: Verso.

Prideaux, S. (2005) *Not So New Labour: A Sociological Critique of New Labour's Policy and Practice*, Bristol: The Polity Press.

Pulignano, V., Stewart, P., Danford, A., and A.M. Richardson, A.M. (eds) (2008) *Flexibility at Work: Developments in the International Automobile Industry*, Basingstoke and New York: Palgrave MacMillan .

Rae, J.B. (1965) *The American Automobile: A Brief History*, The University of Chicago and London: University of Chicago Press.

Reich, R. (2008) *Supercapitalism: The Battle for Democracy in an Age of Big Business*, Cambridge: Icon Books.

Reich, S. (1990) *The Fruits of Fascism: Postwar Prosperity in Historical Perspective*, Ithaca and London: Cornell University Press.

Rowthorn, R.E. and Wells, J.R. (1987) *De-industrialization and Foreign Trade*, Cambridge: Cambridge University Press.

Ruigrock, W. and Van Tulder, R. (1995) *The Logic of International Restructuring*, London and New York: Routledge.

Samuelson, P. (1997) 'Wherein do the European and American Models Differ?'Address delivered at the bank of Italy, October 7, 1997, Number 320, mimeo.

Sawyer, M. (2003) 'The Private Finance Initiative: A Critical Assessment', in D. Coffey and C. Thornley (eds) *Industrial and Labour Market Policy and Performance: Issues and Perspectives*, Routledge: London and New York, 171–189.

Sawyer, M. (2005) 'The Private Finance Initiative: The UK Experience', *Procurement and Financing of Motorways in Europe, Research in Transportation Economics*, Vol. 15: 239–253.

Sawyer, M. and O'Donnell, K. (1999) *A Future for Public Ownership*, London: Lawrence & Wishart (published in association with UNISON).

Shenhav, Y. (1999) *Manufacturing Rationality: The Engineering Foundations of the Managerial Revolution*, New York: Oxford University Press.

Singh, A. (1977) 'UK Industry and the World Economy: A Case of De-Industrialization', *Cambridge Journal of Economics*, Vol. 1, No. 2 (June): 113–136.

Theodore, N. (2007) 'New Labour at Work: Long-term Unemployment and the Geography of Opportunity', *Cambridge Journal of Economics*, Vol. 31, No. 6: 927–939.

Thompson, E.P. (1993) *Customs in Common*, Harmondsworth: Penguin Books.

Thomson, A. (1983) 'The Contexts of Management Behaviour in Industrial Relations in the Public and Private Sectors', in K. Thurley and S. Wood (eds), *Industrial Relations and Management Strategy*, Cambridge: Cambridge University Press.

Thornley, C. (1995) 'The Model Employer Myth: The Need for Theoretical Renewal in Public Sector Industrial Relations', 13th Annual Labour Process Conference, mimeo.

Thornley, C. (1996) 'Segmentation and Inequality in the Nursing Workforce: Re-evaluating the Evaluation of Skills', in R. Crompton, D. Gallie, and K. Purcell (eds) *Changing Forms of Employment: Organisations, Skills and Gender*, London: Routledge, 160–181.

Thornley, C. (1998) *A Question of Fairness: Nurses' Pay Trends 1979–98*, London: UNISON (Evidence to the Review Body for Nurses).

Thornley, C. (2001) 'Divisions in Health-Care Labour', in C. Komaromy (ed.) *Dilemmas in UK Health Care*, Buckingham: Open University Press, 85–107.

Thornley, C. (2003) 'Labour Market Policy and Inequality in the UK', in D. Coffey and C. Thornley (eds) *Industrial and Labour Market Policy and Performance: Issues and Perspectives,* London and New York: Routledge, 83–108.

Thornley, C. (2003a) *Cold Comfort: The State of Local Government Pay and 'More Cold Comfort',* A UNISON briefing for the NJC Local Government Pay Commission, April, London: UNISON.

Thornley, C. (2004) *Perceptions at Work: Women and Men in Local Government,* London: UNISON, 1–64.

Thornley, C. (2005) *Still Waiting? Non-registered Nurses in the NHS, an Update,* London: UNISON (Evidence to the Review Body for Nurses).

Thornley, C. (2006) 'Unequal and Low Pay In the Public Sector', *Industrial Relations Journal,* Vol. 37, No. 4 July: 344–358.

Thornley, C. (2007a) 'Redefining "Modernization"? UNISON and Equality Bargaining in the UK Public Services', Gender, Work and Organisation, 5th International Interdisciplinary Conference, Keele (June).

Thornley, C. (2007b) 'Working Part-time for the State: Gender, Class and the Public Sector Pay Gap', *Gender, Work and Organization,* Issue 14.5, September: 454–475.

Thornley, C. (2008) 'Efficiency and Equity Considerations in the Employment of Health Care Assistants and Support Workers', *Social Policy and Society,* Vol. 7, No. 2: 135–146.

Thornley, C., Ironside, M., and Seifert, R. (2000) 'UNISON and Changes in Collective Bargaining in Health and Local Government', in M. Terry (ed.) *Redefining Public Service Unionism,* London: Routledge, 137–154.

Tolliday, S. (2003) 'The Decline of Ford in Britain: Marketing and Production in Retreat, 1980–2003', in H. Bonin, Y. Lung, and S. Tolliday (eds) *Ford: The European History 1903–2003,* Volume 2, Paris: Editions P.L.A.G.E., 73–152.

Tomlinson, P.R. (2002) 'The Real Effects of Transnational Activity upon Investment and Labour Demand within Japan's Machinery Industries', *International Review of Applied Economics,* Vol. 16, No. 2: 107–129.

Toynbee, P. (2003) *Hard Work: Life in Low-Pay Britain,* London: Bloomsbury.

Tyson, L. (1992) *Who's Bashing Whom? Trade Conflict in High-Technology Industries,* Washington, DC: Institute for International Economics.

Webb, S. and Webb, B. (1897) *Industrial Democracy,* London: Longmans, Green & Co.

Werner, R.A. (2007) 'The Cause of Japan's Recession and the Lessons for the World', in D. Bailey, D. Coffey, and P.R. Tomlinson (eds) *Crisis or Recovery in Japan: State and Industrial Economy,* Cheltenham and Northampton, MA: Edward Elgar.

Wilkinson, F. (2007) 'Neo-liberalism and New Labour Policy: Economic Performance, Historical Comparisons and Future Prospects', *Cambridge Journal of Economics,* Vol. 31, No. 6, November: 817–844.

Wilks, S. (1984) *Industrial Policy and the Motor Industry,* Manchester: Manchester University Press.

Williams, K., Haslam, C., Williams, J., Cutler, T., Adcroft, A., and Johal, S. (1994) *Cars: Analysis, History, Cases,* Oxford: Berghahn.

Willner, J. (1999) 'Market Structure, Corporate Objectives and Cost Efficiency', in K. Cowling (ed.) *Industrial Policy in Europe: Theoretical Perspectives and Practical Proposals*, London and New York: Routledge, 290–310.

Willner, J. (2003) 'Privatisation: A Sceptical Analysis', in D. Parker and D. Saal (eds) *International Handbook of Privatisation*, Cheltenham: Edward Elgar.

Winchester, D. (1983) 'Industrial Relations in The Public Sector', in G. Bain (ed.) *Industrial Relations in Britain*, Oxford: Blackwell.

Womack, P., Jones, D.T., and Roos, D. (1990) *The Machine That Changed the World*, New York: Rawson Associates, MacMillan Publishing Company.

Wood, S. (2001) 'Business, Government, and Patterns of Labor Market Policy in Britain and the Federal Republic of Germany', in P.A. Hall and D. Soskice (eds) *Varieties of Capitalism: The Institutional Foundations of Comparative Advantage*, Oxford: Oxford University Press, 247–274.

Wootton, B. (1955) *The Social Foundations of Wage Policy*, London: George Allen & Unwin.

Wright, T. (1997) *Why Vote Labour?* Harmondsworth: Penguin.

Index